COOKING WITH GIOVANNI CABOTO

Members' Limited Edition

COOKING WITH
GIOVANNI CABOTO

EDITED BY

GIACINTO PIAZZA

PHOTOGRAPHED BY

MAURO CHECHI

BIBLIOASIS

Library and Archives Canada Cataloguing in Publication

Cooking with Giovanni Caboto / the Giovanni Caboto Club ; edited by Giacinto Piazza ; photographed by Mauro Chechi.

Includes index.
ISBN 978-1-926845-97-5

1. Cooking, Italian. 2. Cookbooks. I. Piazza, Giacinto, 1951- II. Giovanni Caboto Club

TX723.C65 2012   641.5945   C2012-905076-8

PRINTED AND BOUND IN CANADA

CONTENTS

Foreword

MANY OF YOU, I am sure, remember waking up Sunday morning to incredible aromas coming from the kitchen. More often than not, Sunday, along with those other holidays, found Mom in the kitchen preparing the afternoon meal that would be enjoyed after church. Whatever region of Italy you are from, Italians share this one common belief: Sunday is family time. Whether it is with your immediate family or together with extended family, Sunday is a day to be shared with others.

We all have our own stories to tell when taking on a project that we can reflect on with family and friends. I've never considered myself a great cook, though I am a passionate one; there is little doubt, however, that working on this cookbook has improved my culinary skills. Learning how to prepare and being able to taste a small portion of regional Italian cuisine over the past 18 months has taken me on an incredible journey through Italy from which I will reap continual benefits. The production of this book was a love affair with food, though I faced many trials and challenges.

During the course of compiling these recipes, a great deal of knowledge was gained about the many variations of Italian cuisine. I learned that a simple pasta dish with fresh tomato sauce will differ when prepared from one region to another. One of our contributors, John Benotto from Veneto, states the tomatoes from his region make their sauce better than any other; another contributor, Remo Tortola from Molise, disagrees and argues that the tomatoes grown in the soil of his region have a better taste. They would inevitably end their discussion with "*Va Bene!*" Of course, they were both right and "*it is okay!*"

What became apparent is that Italians are just as passionate about their food as they are about family, football (soccer) and politics. Sometimes I am unsure about which topic they are most passionate! One thing is for sure: gather two (you only need two) or more Italians, sit them down for a meal and let the fun begin.

The purpose of this book is to offer a gastronomical regional survey of Italian cuisine, colourfully illustrated in over 200 recipes from the homes of our members, their families and friends.

I do hope you take the opportunity to try these recipes with your favourite bottle of Italian wine. A quick final note about wine pairing with your meals: wine tastes better in the company of friends and family. My belief: drink what you enjoy and not what you are told to pair it with. If your palate says, "*I like it,*" then drink it!

Giacinto (Gino) Piazza,
Montallegro, Agrigento, Sicily
(Editor and Chair)

Introduction

ITALIAN COOKING IS AN ART IN ITS OWN WAY. Like a painter who adds an extra dab of this or that, changing the colour by degrees here and there, Italian cooking is similar. The way our mothers and grandmothers cook without ever needing to measure is an art in itself.

In saying that, here are some basic things to keep in mind before attempting any recipe.

The very first step in cooking is to read the recipe all the way through, a few times, from beginning to end. This way you will learn if you have all of the ingredients and tools on hand. You will also be able to look up terms you do not understand so the cooking process flows smoothly.

Most of the recipes start with the ingredient list, and the ingredients are normally listed in the order they are used, sometimes specifying the main ingredient first.

Exact measurements in some of these recipes are essential, though personal taste normally overrides them. When a recipe calls for a tablespoon or teaspoon, we mean for you to use actual measuring utensils, not spoons that you use for eating and serving, though by all means add a pinch here and there if you feel a recipe requires it.

Even the order of the words in an ingredient list changes the preparation of the recipe. For instance, if a recipe calls for *1 cup parsley (chopped fine)*, that is different from *1 cup finely chopped parsley*. In the first case, you should measure 1 cup of fresh parsley, then chop it. In the second case, the parsley should be chopped first, and then measured. The bracket placement changes the measuring technique.

Warm oil means placing the oil in the skillet or pot, turning on the heat and leaving it on the heat for 1 to 2 minutes, until you can feel the warmth of the oil.

After you have read the recipe, gather all the ingredients, pots, pans, bowls, and measuring utensils you will need. Go slowly and double-check all the steps and ingredients.

The body of the recipe contains the instructions about combining, heating and cooking the ingredients.

Cooking a recipe does not have to be complicated or confusing. Ensuring that you are familiar with the recipe and its ingredients will make for a great meal and an enjoyable experience.

Now that you have the book, commit yourself to trying all the recipes within the next year, while sipping your favourite glass of Italian wine, and add your personal touches as you go along.

Salute!
Gino and Mauro

Roberto L. Tonial, President, Giovanni Caboto Club

IN 2011, THE GIOVANNI CABOTO CLUB Art and Culture Committee approached the Board of Directors with the idea to create a cookbook that would represent all the regions of Italy, and would look to collect recipes both from our homes here in Canada and, more importantly, from the kitchens that many of our members left when they emigrated from Italy. These recipes represent a cultural snapshot and could provide everyone a true taste of Italy. Italian Culture has been a foundation of Western Civilization for thousands of years, creating and influencing the modern world in art, music, science and medicine, but it is perhaps in the area of the culinary arts that Italy has the most universal appeal. You may argue on behalf of the merits of Da Vinci, Galileo, or Puccini, but no one can argue that the best food is Italian food, because for Italians, every dish is a masterpiece, every meal is a banquet and every gathering is a celebration of family and friends!

It was with this in mind that a small group of volunteers were tasked with reaching out to the Members of the Caboto Club to secure their favourite recipes. While this may sound like a simple task, keep in mind that most of those recipes are closely guarded secrets. We will always share a dish, but get-ting that secret ingredient or that special spice that makes the dish so good is not the easiest thing to do. All of this would not have been possible without the leadership of Gino Piazza. Gino was not only the Chairman of this group, he was also its driving force, and it was because of his tireless devotion to this idea that you now have this cookbook. Now, as the Giovanni Caboto Club enters its 88th year, it is with great pleasure that we present this culinary tour of Italy to you.

On behalf of the Board of Directors of the Giovanni Caboto Club, I would like to thank all of the members who contributed their most cherished recipes. A special thank you also needs to go out to Gino Piazza and his committee, the Chairman of the Art and Culture Committee, Giuliano Lunardi for his support, Mauro Chechi for his beautiful photographs and of course, to all of you reading this book, as it is for you that all of this effort was undertaken. Try the recipes, experiment with the ingredients and share the results with your friends and family.

Buon Appetito!
(Roberto is a 3rd-generation member
of the club and its 28th president.)

Lasagna di Nonna Elena
(Nonna Elena's Lasagna)

Elena (Presello) Tonial, Fagagna, Udine

Growing up, this was always one of my favourite dishes that my Mom would prepare for us. There was never a more perfect Sunday than one where we had lasagna for dinner. Just before my Mom was diagnosed with Alzheimer's, she gave my daughter all of her "secret" recipes so that they would not be forgotten. I could think of nothing better than to share this with all of you. —Roberto.

(Yield: 8-10 servings)

1 pound lasagna noodles
olive oil for drizzling
WHITE SAUCE:
2 tablespoons butter
2 tablespoons flour

2 cups milk
½ teaspoon freshly grated nutmeg
5-6 cups meat sauce (see page 308)
2 pounds shredded Mozzarella cheese
½ cup grated Parmesan cheese

1. Bring large pot of salted water to boil. Add lasagna noodles and cook for approx. 4 minutes, until softened.

2. Drain into colander and run cold water over noodles to stop cooking process. Place drained noodles in bowl with a little olive oil so they will not stick together. Set aside.

3. Melt butter in small saucepan over medium heat. Add flour and stir until there are no lumps.

4. Slowly add milk, stirring continuously. When mixture comes to a boil, reduce to a simmer and continue stirring until it is well blended.

5. Sprinkle in nutmeg and when well-combined set aside until ready to use (*White Sauce*).

6. Add thin layer of meat sauce into an ungreased 9x13 baking dish and arrange a single layer of noodles.

7. Add another layer of meat sauce, a generous drizzle of white sauce and cover with Mozzarella.

8. Continue building layers in same fashion until all noodles are used up, making sure the last layer is topped with both sauces and remaining Mozzarella and Parmesan cheeses.

9. Cover dish with foil. Bake in oven preheated to 350°F for approx. 45 minutes.

10. Remove foil and allow to bake for another 10 to 15 minutes.

11. Remove from oven and re-cover with foil, allowing it to stand for 10 minutes.

Serve warm and enjoy.

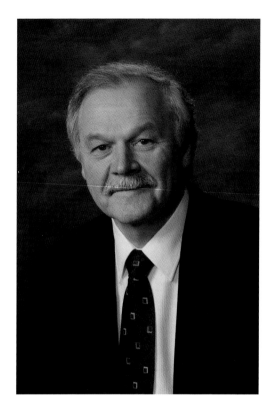

Ron Moro, General Manager, Giovanni Caboto Club

CONGRATULATIONS to Gino Piazza, Mauro Chechi and the "Cookbook" committee on a job well done! The committee, with the help of our cooks at the Giovanni Caboto Club, has cooked each recipe that is presented in this book. Imagine the time, effort and the commitment involved. Quite a remarkable accomplishment!

I have often been asked what makes this cookbook any different from so many others on the market or available online. My response has been short and simple. Yes, you can go online and look up almost any recipe you wish. However, you will not find *any* of these recipes. These recipes are "personal," or "my mother's," or "my grandmother's," recipes that have been handed down from generation to generation. You will not find these anywhere else. These recipes all have one ingredient missing from their ingredient list: "LOVE."

Ron was born in Cusano, Pordenone, Italy and immigrated to Canada with his parents, brother and sister in 1949. Educated in Windsor, Ron received his Bachelor of Arts in 1969, and his MBA in 1971 from the University of Windsor. He was the Founder and President of the Ethnic Clubs Association of Windsor and Essex County, a member of the University of Windsor's Board of Governors from 1979 to 1987, and a member of the United Way Board of Directors from 1976 to 1986, including serving as its President in 1982 and its Campaign's Vice-Chair in 1986. Ron was a founding Board Member of the Trillium Foundation of Ontario (1982-1990) as well as the Italian Vice Counsel from 1989 to 1996. He is the recipient of many awards, including Canada's 125th Commemorative Award of Honour, Windsor-Essex County Italian of the Year Award for 2000, Caboto Club's *Laurea Emeritus Summa Cum Laude Award* in 2005, and the Pordenone, Italy Award for Fidelity of Labour in 2009.

Ron is and has been the General Manager of the Giovanni Caboto Club for over 25 years, has served on the Club's Board of Directors for 16 years, and he was the Club's 21st President for 12 of those years.

Minestra di Fagioli con Muset alla Contadina
(Puréed Bean Soup with Muset – Peasant-Style)

Ron Moro, Cusano, Pordenone

This is a long process and therefore it is best to make a large quantity at a time, which then can be frozen in containers until ready to use. If you prefer to make a smaller quantity, you can divide the ingredients into the proper proportions. The recipe below will make about 378 ounces or 11 quarts.

3 musets (cotechino)
(about 1 pound each with casings)
3 large carrots (diced)
4 celery stalks (diced)
2 onions (diced)
¼ cup finely chopped parsley
1 tablespoon Italian seasoning
1 can Romano beans (19 ounces)
1 can chickpeas (19 ounces)

1 can Red kidney beans (19 ounces)
1 can White kidney beans (19 ounces)
1 can Bean Medley (19 ounces)
10 medium potatoes (peeled and cut in half)
¼ teaspoon Allspice (a pinch)
4 bay leaves
½ garlic head (7 to 8 cloves minced)
1 chicken bouillon cube
1 beef bouillon cube

1. In large pot capable of holding 4 gallons (90 cups), add 44 cups of water and bring to a boil over high heat.

2. Add all of the above ingredients up to and including the garlic. Once soup has returned to a boil, reduce heat to a simmer and cook for approx. 3 hours.

3. After 3 hours, remove all ingredients, remove musets from their casings, emulsify and purée.

4. Pass through sieve and discard any leftovers.

5. Return liquid back into cleaned pot and return to slow boil for approx. 2 hours.

6. While boiling, continuously skim off all oils and fats that come to the surface.

7. When all oil and fat has been skimmed off, crumble and add bouillon cubes and finish cooking.

Prior to serving, add some parboiled rice to the soup, a sprinkle of Parmesan cheese and slices of cooked muset on the side.

Steven Ward, Executive Chef, Giovanni Caboto Club

BORN IN FOLKESTONE, ENGLAND, Steven moved to Alberta, Canada when he was 8 years old. His interest in cooking started at the age of 15 and by the age of 16 he'd landed his first cooking job preparing fast food at Little Bow Provincial Park in Alberta.

At the age of 17 he became a breakfast cook at Huskey's Truck Stop, where he quickly learned the importance of speed and organization.

In 1986, he began his formal training at SAIT (Southern Alberta Institute of Technology), where he completed a 3 year Culinary Arts Program in 1989.

While in school, he was working at a well-known Steak House in Alberta called the "The Longhorn." The Longhorn enabled him to learn about the principals of meat cookery, and it was there that he was taught how to maintain a high level of professionalism in the kitchen.

He moved to Windsor in 1990, where he worked at a few local restaurants before being hired at the Giovanni Caboto Club in April of that year.

At the Caboto Club he worked under the supervision of European Chef Jim Oran, and has been privileged to work with some very talented ladies, including Fedora Rumiel, who had over 30 years "Traditional Italian" cooking experience. There he was taught the true traditional dishes from all regions of Italy.

In 1996 Steven became the Head Chef of the Giovanni Caboto Club, a position that he proudly holds today.

While working at the club, he obtained "The Red Seal" certification in 1996.

One of his career highlights includes cooking for the Olympic Athletes at the 1988 Winter Olympic Games in Calgary. He also had, while working at the Longhorn, the thrill of cooking and meeting some of his favourite hockey players, including Lanny McDonald, Joe Nieuwendyk, Theo Flury and Doug Gilmore.

Here at the Giovanni Caboto Club he has had the privilege of preparing meals for several local celebrities, MPPs, MPs, and Canada's Prime Minister, as well as celebrities such as Henry Winkler, Wayne Gretzky and Jason Spezza, just to name a few.

Currently, Steven and his team take great pride in creating a memorable culinary experience for our brides and grooms, as well as for all of our guests at the Giovanni Caboto Club.

The opportunity to work on Cooking with Giovanni Caboto *gave me a greater understanding of how regional foods differ with their use of ingredients and cooking techniques. After working 20-plus years in professional kitchens, it was truly a pleasure to experience the simplicity and incredible flavours of family recipes that were handed down from one generation to another.*

Enjoy,
Steven!

Pasta Mare e Monte
(Pasta with Seafood and Mushrooms)

Steven Ward, Executive Chef, Giovanni Caboto Club

(Yield: 4 to 6 servings)

5 cups tomato sauce (page 308)
3 tablespoons vegetable oil
3 cups mixed Portobello and Cremini mushrooms
2 cups each, scallops, white fish
32 ounces baby clams in juice
1 pound fettuccine
(or pasta of your choice)

Salad shrimp, medium shrimp
(31 to 40 size, de-veined and tail off)
1 pound mussels (cleaned)
salt and freshly ground pepper
chili flakes (to taste)
1 cup roughly chopped fresh Italian parsley
2 teaspoons corn starch and water
as a thickener (if needed)

1. Bring large pot of salted water to boil.

2. In large saucepan, bring tomato sauce to boil and then lower to a simmer.

3. Warm oil in skillet over medium heat. Sauté mushrooms for 5 to 7 minutes, then add them to tomato sauce.

4. Add scallops, fish, clams and clam juice to tomato sauce and continue cooking for another 5 minutes, stirring often.

5. Add pasta to boiling water and cook until al dente.

6. Add shrimp to tomato sauce and cook for another 5 to 7 minutes.

7. Once fish is tender and flaky, add mussels and cook for another 2 to 3 minutes.

8. Season with salt, pepper and chili flakes (to taste).

9. Drain pasta and place into serving bowl. Add sauce and mix.

10. Garnish with parsley and serve immediately!

Note: Discard any mussels that have not opened.

Chef Remo Tortola, Giovanni Caboto Club Pizzeria

I WAS HONOURED WHEN ASKED to contribute to this book. Italian food from different regions is an adventure in itself. All I can say is, *mangiare* (eat)!

I grew up in my parents' home, along with my brother and sister, in a little picturesque village (Miranda, Isernia, Molise) that rises on a small hill at the foot of Mount Pietrereie. Although my family owned a restaurant, my schooling was in architectural design. Only later in life was I drawn towards the culinary side of things, and it was not until 1997 that I decided to open a restaurant/pizzeria.

I married my childhood sweetheart, Maria Pia, and in 2002 came to Canada. In 2008, our son Francesco blessed the household.

In 2003 the Caboto Club's Pizzeria was opened, and in partnership with the club we have made so many wonderful pizzas, and have never been afraid to experiment with an individual's personal taste.

This partnership has enabled me to expand the pizzeria by adding a "We will bring our oven to You!" feature which has proved very successful.

Our wood-burning oven gives a very special texture and cooked flavour to the pizzas.

The following is our basic recipe for pizza in your home. Even taking into consideration the use of a gas/electric oven, this should produce a wonderful pizza.

There are only two other pieces of advice that I can offer:

First, keep experimenting until you have perfected the dough; and, second, use the best quality and freshest ingredients.

Buon Appetito,
Remo!

The Basic Pizza

Remo Tortola, Chef, Giovanni Caboto Club Pizzeria

If time permits, allow the dough in step #2 to sit overnight in the fridge. Remember the best pizzas come with the use of the freshest ingredients. Enjoy and experiment.

Yield: 2, 10 to 12 inch pizza servings
2½ cups all-purpose flour (extra for dusting)
1 cup water (cold water in the summer/
room temperature in the winter)

2 teaspoons dry yeast or 4 teaspoons fresh yeast
3 teaspoons salt
5 tablespoons extra-virgin olive oil
whole-wheat flour (pizza peel)

Step #1 – Making the dough

1. Pile flour on work surface and form a well, then add water to the well.

2. On one side of the well add dry yeast, on the opposite side add salt. Add oil in the centre of the well.

3. Mix all ingredients until dough starts to pull away from your hands. Knead dough until a smooth ball is formed (20 to 25 minutes).

4. Divide dough into 2 pieces and re-form into balls.

Step #2 – The Risen Effect

1. Coat two separate bowls with oil and place a ball of dough in each bowl. Coat each ball with a little more oil.

2. Seal each bowl with plastic wrap and refrigerate for at least 24 hours. This will allow for a crunchier crust (if using right away, allow the dough to rise, doubling in size, for 2 to 3 hours at room temperature).

Step #3 – Prepare and Cook

1. Preheat oven to 500°F with pizza-stone (in oven).

2. Remove dough from fridge, making sure it has doubled in size.

3. Mound plenty of extra flour on work surface and place one ball on it. Press down, stretching (not rolling) to the desired size. While bottom is coated with flour, flip dough over and repeat on the other side to a ¼-inch thickness.

4. Dust a pizza peel with whole-wheat flour, place shaped dough onto peel, and working quickly dress with the following ingredients for a Margherita pizza (below, in order).

5. Quickly open oven door and insert pizza on the pizza stone, closing door immediately. Cook 5 to 8 minutes.

6. Remove, slice and enjoy while hot!

Margherita Pizza: tomato sauce, whole basil leaves, Mozzarella cheese. This is the simplest and most basic; experiment with your favourite toppings. Dusting the pizza peel with whole-wheat flour allows consistent cooking, where regular flour tends to burn quickly.

(L to R): Herb Girard, Natalie Girard, Chef Steve Ward,
Domenico Teti, Nick Paré

Kitchen Staff

"Working on the cookbook was interesting, fun and educational." —Herb

"It was truly enjoyable learning about the ethnicity of Italian cuisine." —Natalie

"What I enjoyed most about working on the cookbook was tasting how the flavours
of the food change from region to region." —Domenic

"It was a truly fascinating experience to learn about the different regions of Italy
through their food." —Nick

Cestino di Formaggi
(Asiago and Parmigiano~Reggiano Cheese Bowls)

Domenico Teti, Giovanni Caboto Club

(Yield: 6 five-inch bowls)

2 cups shredded Asiago cheese
2½ cups grated Parmigiano-Reggiano cheese
4 tablespoons white flour
parchment paper
6 ceramic or stainless steel bowls (about 5 inch diameter)

1. In a bowl, combine cheeses and flour and mix until all the cheese is coated with flour. Put mixture in a fine strainer and shake off excess flour.

2. Layer a cookie sheet with parchment paper and spread cheese mixture into a flat disc shape large enough to cover the bottom and sides of one ceramic bowl. Repeat until you have 6 discs.

3. Bake in oven preheated to 400°F until lightly golden (between 5 to 10 min).

4. With all the bowls upside down, coat lightly with cooking spray.

5. When cheese discs have cooked, work quickly to lift gently with a large spatula and place one on top of each bowl.

6. If the cheese discs do not shape themselves, gently mold them around bowls.

7. Place bowls in fridge to cool for approx. 10 minutes. Once cooled, remove the formed cheese bowls.

8. If using immediately, fill with your favourite risotto, salad or anything you like just prior to serving. If not, return to the fridge until ready for use.

We used stainless steel bowls to make the shape, but use your imagination and use anything that will give it an appropriate shape. The cheese bowls can be made a day or two ahead and kept in the fridge until ready to fill.

TRENTINO ALTO-ADIGE

CAPITAL

Trento

RED WINE

Teroldego Rotaliano

WHITE WINE

Taminer Aromatico

Stracciatella
(Egg-drop Soup)

Bruna Zambelli, Volano, Trento

(Yield: 4 servings)

4 eggs
4 tablespoons grated Parmesan cheese
2 teaspoons fresh parsley (finely chopped)
6 cups chicken or beef broth
salt and pepper to taste

1. Whisk eggs, cheese and parsley together in bowl.

2. In saucepan over medium heat, warm broth. Once it has come to a boil, reduce heat to low and simmer for approx. 10 minutes.

3. Slowly add egg-cheese-parsley mixture to broth and mix well using whisk. Allow to simmer for 4 to 5 minutes.

4. Stir occasionally, especially immediately prior to serving, to avoid large clumps.

Serve immediately.

Boiling water with beef or chicken bouillon and a pinch of butter can be a substitute for homemade broth.

Minestrone D'Orzo
(Pearl Barley Soup)

Natalia (Odorizzi) Pinamonti, Tuenno, Trento

(Yield: 4 servings)

1 cup barley
8 cups water
3 potatoes (diced)
2 carrots (diced)
2 celery stalks (diced)
2 vegetable bouillon cubes
salt and freshly ground pepper
2 tablespoons extra-virgin olive oil

1. Rinse barley and add to saucepan with water, potatoes, carrots and celery. Cook over medium-high heat.

2. Once it comes to a boil, reduce heat to low and let soup simmer for 1 hour.

3. Add vegetable bullion to soup and continue to simmer slowly for an additional hour, stirring occasionally.

4. At the end, adjust to taste by adding salt and freshly ground pepper.

Before serving drizzle with extra-virgin olive oil.

This is a good soup for a cold winter day. Serve with Italian crusty bread. This soup tastes even better when reheated the day after.

Minestra di Trippa
(Tripe Soup)

Lia (Giovanella) Ballardini, Preore, Trento

(Yield: 4 servings)

1¼ pounds *Trippa*
2 tablespoons each, extra-virgin
olive oil and butter
2 potatoes (cubed ¾-inch)
1 cup borlotti beans

2 carrots (cubed ½-inch)
¼ head savoy cabbage (finely chopped)
1 celery stalk (chopped ½-inch pieces)
salt and freshly ground pepper (to taste)
¼ cup grated Parmesan cheese

1. Wash tripe well, and boil for 1 hour in salted water.

2. Remove tripe (discard the water) and cut into thin strips (¼-inch).

3. Warm oil and butter in large saucepan over medium heat; cook tripe for 3 to 4 minutes.

4. Add all vegetables (potatoes, beans, carrots, cabbage, and celery).

5. Season with salt and pepper and add enough water to cover contents in the saucepan.

6. Bring to boil and then reduce heat to a simmer. Cook partially covered for 2 to 3 hours, adding water as required.

Serve with grated Parmesan cheese.

Zuppa di Pane della Val D'Ultimo
(Flatbread Soup)

Lorenzo Facchinato, Bolzano

(Yield: 4 servings)

6 tablespoons extra-virgin olive oil
1 large onion (sliced into ¼-inch rings)
4 ounces speck (bacon, sliced into ¼-inch strips)
4½ tablespoons flour
4 cups water or beef broth

1 bay leaf
1 pinch of cumin (¹/8 teaspoon)
1 teaspoon salt
slices of toasted bread
1 tablespoon extra-virgin olive oil

1. In skillet, heat 3 tablespoons oil over medium heat. Cook onions and speck until onions are translucent.

2. In another skillet over low heat, add remaining oil and flour and cook slowly until it has turned lightly golden. Add water, bay leaf, cumin, salt and stir well.

3. Once it has come to a simmer, pass through a sieve and add to the onions and speck. Bring to a boil, cooking for another 5 minutes.

4. Serve with toasted bread rolls or flatbread drizzled with extra-virgin olive oil.

Suggestion: When toasting the flour you can add a little butter.

Tortel di Patate
(Potato Pie)

Graziosa (Agnello) Pedrazzoli, Rovereto, Trento

This recipe came from the *Circolo Trentino Windsor-Detroit Cookbook*, submitted by Mary Petroni. She indicated it was her mother's recipe, Graziosa Pedrazzoli.

(Yield: 4 servings)

5 large white potatoes (peeled)
½ cup all-purpose flour
2 eggs beaten

salt and freshly ground pepper (to taste)
3 tablespoons extra-virgin olive oil
3 tablespoons butter (cold)

1. Grate potatoes using large-hole side of grater.

2. Squeeze grated potatoes in towel to remove excess liquid, and place potatoes in large bowl.

3. Add flour, eggs, salt and pepper. Mix well.

4. Grease 10x15 cookie sheet with oil and pour potato mixture into cookie sheet. Mixture should be approx. ½-inch thick.

5. Dot the top of the mixture with pieces of butter (¼-inch cubes).

6. Bake in oven preheated to 375°F until golden brown (approx. 1 hour).

Cut into triangular pieces and serve as an addition to any meal.

Risotto con Funghi
(Mushroom Risotto)

Alfreda Gorder, Trento

(Yield: 6 servings)

¾ cup dried sliced porcini mushrooms
6 cups heated vegetable broth
5 tablespoons extra-virgin olive oil
3½ tablespoons butter
1 large onion (diced)

1½ cups arborio or carnaroli Italian rice
1/3 cup dry white wine
1 cup grated Parmigiano cheese
1 teaspoon salt
fresh chopped parsley (to taste)

1. Bring dried porcini mushrooms and 1 cup of broth to boil in small saucepan over medium heat. Cook 5 to 8 minutes, then set aside.

2. Warm oil and butter in large skillet over medium heat. Add onions and sauté until translucent.

3. Add rice and stir for approx. 2 minutes. Add white wine and stir well until wine has evaporated.

4. Add contents from the saucepan containing the mushrooms and the broth to rice. Allow to come to a boil.

5. As the rice absorbs the liquid, continue to add hot broth ½ cup at a time while continuing to stir. Do not let rice become too dry.

6. Cook until al dente (approx. 25 to 30 minutes), over medium-to-low heat. Do not overcook.

7. At the very end of the cooking time, add grated cheese and stir well to melt the cheese until the texture becomes creamy.

8. Remove from heat, season to taste and stir in chopped parsley.

Serve immediately.

Best enjoyed hot. Cheese lovers: feel free to add more cheese to the plated dish. Porcini mushrooms are bountiful in the mountains of Trentino from July to September.

Strangolapreti
(Spinach Gnocchi)

Anna Negri, Tres, Trento

The Trentino term for green gnocchi, Strangolapreti, literally means priest-choker or strangler. This dish has been a part of traditional cuisine since the era of the Council of Trent. Indeed, it derives from "strozzapreti" (a dish of Tuscan origin), adapted because it was the favourite food of the prelates during the Council held in Trento between 1545 and 1563.

2 pounds dry day-old bread
(cut into ½-inch cubes)
2 cups milk (warmed, not boiled)
1 pound fresh spinach
½ cup butter
salt and freshly ground pepper
½ teaspoon grated nutmeg

2 tablespoons extra-virgin olive oil
1 small onion (finely diced)
½ cup grated Grana cheese
2 eggs
3 tablespoons flour
10-15 sage leaves

1. Soak bread in tepid milk for approx. three hours.

2. Boil spinach in salted water. Drain and squeeze out as much liquid as possible. Chop fine.

3. In skillet over medium heat, add half the butter (¼ cup) and sauté spinach.

4. Season with pepper and nutmeg. Set aside to cool.

5. In the same skillet, over medium heat, add oil and sauté the onion until translucent. Set aside to cool.

6. Add half the grated Grana cheese (¼ cup), the eggs, ½ tablespoon salt, flour, the cooled onions and spinach to a bowl. Blend well.

7. Make the Strangolapreti by rolling the dough into small balls or the classic gnocchi shape.

8. Add Strangolapreti to pot of boiling salted water. They are cooked when they float to the surface.

9. Drain well and serve with a generous sprinkling of remaining Grana cheese and sage-seasoned melted butter.

Note to season sage: in a small skillet, over low heat, melt the rest of the butter, add the sage and cook until sage becomes slightly crispy and butter begins to turn brown.

Cappuccio in Umido
(Stewed Cabbage with Meat)

Giuditta Zadra, Tres, Trento

(Yield: 4 servings)

4 tablespoons extra-virgin olive oil
1 medium onion (diced)
1 large cabbage (sliced very thin)
½ pound smoked bacon (sliced ½-inch thick)

1 pound fresh sausage (see note)
1 pound smoked pork meat
or spare ribs (see note)
6 cups chicken or beef broth (warmed)

1. Warm oil in large oven-proof Dutch oven over medium heat and sauté onions until translucent.

2. Add cabbage and smoked bacon with enough broth to cover contents.

3. Cook for approx. 10 minutes, making sure the Dutch oven does not dry out. Add broth as required.

4. Remove from stove and place Dutch oven in an oven preheated to 350°F.

5. The entire baking time will be 2 hours. During the final half hour add sausage and other smoked pork meat.

6. Add broth as required, until the last ½ hour.

7. The cabbage dish is done when the cabbage begins to turn light brown, the broth has boiled down, and the meat is cooked.

8. Serve this dish with polenta (see page 308).

Note: the sausage and ribs should be cut into small pieces and then boiled in water separately on the stove for approx. ½ hour to cook partially and to eliminate the grease.

Canederli
(Bread Balls)

Irma (Negri) Geri, Casez, Trento

The Trentino-Alto Adige is a mountainous region, with numerous valleys running down the mountain to the central Adige Valley. The old recipes were based on the agricultural produce of the mountain, and are therefore simple and genuine.

Today they use olive oil as a common ingredient; however the original recipes called for lard and butter. A few recipes use kitchen leftovers with the addition of common household ingredients found in most rural kitchens. This original Canederli recipe is the classic recipe using leftover stale bread. Today many other versions of the Canederli recipe can be found in both the Alto-Adige and Trentino Provinces.

(Yield: 4 servings)

1 pound stale bread (cut into ½-inch cubes)
2 cups milk (warmed, not boiled)
4 eggs
2 fresh sausages (Note: Trentino style)
¼ pound smoked bacon (cut very fine or
substitute with speck or cooked ham)
¼ cup fresh parsley (chopped fine)
½ cup grated Parmesan cheese
salt and freshly ground pepper
3 tablespoons flour
breadcrumbs or flour to coat
the outside of the canederli balls
8 cups chicken or beef broth

1. In a large bowl, add cubed bread into the warm milk and soak for one hour.

2. Add eggs and browned sausage. Mix well.

3. Add bacon, chopped parsley and grated cheese. Season with salt and pepper and add 3 tablespoons flour. Mix well.

4. When ingredients have amalgamated, use your hands to make balls to the size you would like (Suggestion – up to tennis-ball size).

5. Roll lightly in flour or breadcrumbs.

6. In large saucepan over medium heat, bring broth to a boil.

7. Add the canederli balls to boiling broth. Cook for 15 to 20 minutes.

Serve the canederli in the broth.

You can also serve the canederli without broth, with melted butter and grated Parmesan cheese added to the top, or with goulash and sauerkraut.

Note: Trentino style means the casing is removed and the meat is browned separately in a skillet for 3 to 5 minutes.

Spezzatino e Polenta
(Beef and Pork Stew with Polenta)

Aurora (Zadra) Negri, Tres, Trento

(Yield: 6 servings)

3 tablespoons extra-virgin olive oil
(or butter)
1 medium onion (finely chopped)
1 sprig rosemary
8-10 sage leaves
1 garlic clove (finely chopped)
1 pound each, stewing beef and pork
(cut into 1½- to 2-inch cubes)

1 teaspoon coarse salt
freshly ground pepper (to taste)
2 tablespoons butter
3 tablespoons flour
2 cups broth
(water and beef bullion can be substituted)
2 tablespoons tomato paste
fresh herbs to garnish

1. Warm oil (or butter) in large oven-proof Dutch oven over medium heat. Sauté onions, rosemary, sage and garlic in olive oil until onions are golden brown (approx. 5 minutes).

2. Discard rosemary and sage, add stewing beef and pork. Brown meat well (approx. 4 minutes each side). Add salt and pepper and set aside.

3. Melt butter in small saucepan over low heat. Add flour, stirring constantly until it is light-to-medium brown.

4. Gradually add broth and tomato paste, stirring constantly until flour is totally dissolved.

5. Add this liquid to the meat in Dutch oven, stir well and cook for 2 more minutes. Transfer to an oven preheated to 350°F and roast for 1½ hours. If mixture becomes too dry or thick, add additional broth. Stir 1 or 2 times during cooking time.

Serve with polenta (see page 308) and garnish with fresh herbs.

Coniglio alla Trentina con Polenta
(Rabbit with Polenta)

Anna Cavosi, Trento

(Yield: 5 servings)

1 rabbit cut into pieces
(finely cut liver)
¼ cup extra-virgin olive oil
3½ tablespoons butter
½ teaspoons salt and
freshly ground pepper (to taste)
1 cup dry white wine

SAUCE:
¼ cup extra-virgin olive oil
1 onion (diced)
1 carrot (diced)
1 stalk celery (diced)
1 sprig rosemary
4 cups chicken broth (warmed)

1. Warm oil and butter in large saucepan over medium heat. Braise rabbit (keep the liver out).

2. Add salt and pepper. Add white wine in small amounts, until all the meat is well browned. Reduce heat to low and let rabbit simmer covered for approx. 1 hour. Make sure rabbit remains moist by adding broth as needed.

3. Make sauce by heating ¼ cup of oil in skillet over medium heat. Sauté onions, carrots, celery, rosemary and finely chopped liver for approx. 10 minutes. (If sauce becomes too thick, add a small quantity of broth.)

4. Remove rosemary sprig and put mixture in blender for approx. 30 seconds.

5. Add sauce to the rabbit after it has simmered for approx. 1 hour (as indicated above).

6. Continue to cook over low heat until meat starts to detach from bone (approx. another ½ hour). Add broth as required.

This dish is best enjoyed with polenta (see page 308).

VENETO

CAPITAL

Venezia

RED WINE

Amarone della Valpolicella

WHITE WINE

Soave Bianco

Valle D'Aosta

Piemonte

Lombardia

Trentino-Alto Adige

Friuli-Venezia Giulia

Veneto

Liguria

Emilia-Romagna

Ligurian Sea

Toscana

Marche

Umbria

Adriatic Sea

Abruzzo

Lazio

Molise

Campania

Puglia

Basilicata

Sardegna

Calabria

Tyrrhenian Sea

Mediterranean Sea

Sicilia

Ionian Sea

Risotto e Asparagi
(Asparagus Risotto)

Dennis Segatto, Gaiarine, Treviso

(Yield: 4 servings)

1 tablespoon extra-virgin olive oil
½ pound asparagus
(trimmed and cut 1-inch)
1 medium onion
(diced)
1½ cups arborio rice

½ cup white wine
4 cups hot chicken stock
(plus more as needed)
3 tablespoons unsalted butter
3 tablespoons grated Parmesan cheese
sea salt and freshly ground pepper

1. Warm oil in skillet over medium heat and sauté asparagus and onions for approx. 5 minutes. Remove from heat and set aside.

2. In a Dutch oven over medium heat add the rice. Stir occasionally. Toast dry until rice is translucent (2 to 3 minutes, watching so as not to brown).

3. Add wine and continue stirring until all the wine has evaporated.

4. Add heated chicken stock until rice is fully covered. Continue stirring until stock has been totally absorbed.

5. Continue adding more stock a cup at a time, and continue stirring until most of the chicken stock has been incorporated.

6. When rice is al dente, add sautéed asparagus and onions and cook for another 2 to 3 minutes.

7. Turn off heat and stir in butter and cheese. Season with salt and pepper.

Serve immediately.

Pasta al Pesto
(Pasta with Parsley/Basil Pesto)

Nereo Favrin, Loria, Treviso

(Yield: 4 servings)

1 pound penne
(or your favourite pasta)
¼ cup parsley
(fresh and tightly packed)
¼ cup basil
(fresh and tightly packed)

3 ounces Feta or favourite cheese
3 garlic cloves
(peeled)
4 tablespoons pine nuts
2 cups extra-virgin olive oil
salt and freshly ground pepper

1. Clean parsley and basil and dry thoroughly.

2. Using a food processor, pulse the parsley. Add basil and pulse a few times until well mixed.

3. Add cheese, garlic and pine nuts and pulse a few more times until well mixed.

4. Add oil from the top of the processor a little at a time until you get a smooth mixture.

5. After you have cooked and drained your favourite pasta (reserving approx. 1 cup of the cooking liquid), add 3 to 4 tablespoons of pesto and mix well. Add some of the cooking liquid if it is too dry.

6. Season with salt and pepper.

Serve immediately, topped with more cheese.

Note: The remaining pesto can be held in the fridge for approx. 1 week. It can be placed in a tightly sealed container (such as a freezer jar) and frozen up to 1 month.

Salsa con Fagioli alla Vicentina
(Bean Salad)

Luigi Chemello, Romano d'Ezzelino, Vicenza

(Yield: 6 servings)

3 tablespoons extra-virgin olive oil

1 tablespoons butter

1 medium onion (diced)

2 salted anchovies
(cut in small pieces)

1 tablespoon finely chopped fresh parsley

1 tablespoon white vinegar

1 teaspoon sugar

½ teaspoon freshly grated nutmeg

1 pound cooked white kidney beans
(cooled to room temperature)

salt and pepper for seasoning

1. Warm oil and butter in skillet over medium heat. Sauté onions until translucent. Add anchovies and parsley and cook for approx. 15 minutes.

2. Remove from heat and allow to cool at room temperature.

3. Combine the cooled mixture, vinegar, sugar and nutmeg in a large bowl. Season with salt and pepper.

4. Add beans and serve as a side dish at room temperature.

Peperonata
(Stewed Vegetables)

John Benotto, Conegliano, Treviso

(Yield: 4 servings)

¼ cup extra-virgin olive oil	2 green peppers
1 onion (diced)	(chopped ¾-inch wide and 1-inch long)
3 garlic cloves (minced)	14 ounces diced tomatoes
1 large eggplant	1 teaspoon tomato paste
(cubed ¾-inch)	salt and freshly ground pepper
2 zucchini (cubed ¾-inch)	¼ teaspoon sugar
	½ cup parsley (chopped fine)

1. Warm oil in large skillet over medium heat and sauté onions and garlic until onions are translucent.
2. Add eggplant, zucchini and green peppers. Cook for approx. 5 minutes.
3. Add diced tomatoes and paste. Mix until everything is incorporated. Cook for approx. 3 minutes.
4. Season with salt and pepper. Add sugar and parsley. Stir.
5. Cook until vegetables are tender.
6. Season with salt and pepper and serve warm.

This dish can be served by itself as a side dish or mixed with your favourite pasta. You can use yellow or green zucchini or even yellow, orange or red peppers to give this dish a vibrant colour.

Fettucine Mare e Monte con Zafferano
(Fettuccine with Saffron)

John Todesco, Tezze sul Brenta, Vicenza

(Yield: 4 servings)

1 pound fettuccine
MUSHROOM SAUCE:
3 tablespoons extra-virgin olive oil
2 tablespoons butter
salt and freshly ground pepper
8 ounces shitake or oyster
mushrooms (diced)

2 garlic cloves (minced)
¼ cup brandy
SAFFRON SAUCE:
8 ounces 35% cream
1 envelope saffron
8 ounces small shrimp
(shelled and deveined)

1. Warm 1 tablespoon oil with ½ tablespoon butter in large skillet over medium heat. Add mushrooms and garlic. Season with salt and pepper. Sauté until liquid from mushrooms has evaporated (approx. 5 to 8 minutes).

2. Remove skillet from heat. Carefully add brandy and cook until all alcohol has evaporated. Set aside.

3. Add cream and saffron to small saucepan over low heat. Stir until dissolved. Do not boil. Set aside.

4. Warm remaining oil and butter in another skillet over medium heat. Add shrimp and cook for approx. 3 minutes. Season with salt and pepper, then remove shrimp from pan and set aside.

Reduce the remaining liquid to half. Remove from heat and add a little of the saffron mixture. Return shrimp to this mixture and set aside.

5. While preparing the above mixtures, have a large pot of slightly salted water boiling; add the fettuccine and cook until al dente.

6. Drain fettuccine and add it to the skillet with the mushroom mixture. Cook over low heat. Mix well.

7. Add in remaining saffron sauce and the shrimp with its sauce. Mix well.

Serve immediately. If desired, Parmesan cheese can be sprinkled on top before serving.

Coscia di Tacchino alla Vicentina
(Turkey Leg)

Marisa Chemello, Cadola, Belluno

(Yield: 2 servings)

3 tablespoons extra-virgin olive oil	**1 cup chicken broth**
1 turkey leg (substitute 2 large turkey breasts)	**1 chicken bouillon cube (broken up)**
1 tablespoon mustard	**1 rosemary sprig**
1 cup white wine	**salt and freshly ground pepper**

1. Warm 2 tablespoons of oil in large saucepan over medium heat.

2. Brown turkey leg on all sides (approx. 12 to 15 minutes).

3. Meanwhile, add remaining oil to a bowl and whisk in mustard. Brush the mustard mixture over turkey leg. Continue cooking for another 10 minutes.

4. Add wine and cook until the alcohol has evaporated.

5. Add broth, bouillon cube and rosemary. Reduce heat to lowest setting and cook for approx. 1 hour (covered). Add extra broth as necessary to make sure the dish does not dry out.

6. Season with salt and pepper.

Serve immediately.

Risotto con Zucchine
(Risotto with Zucchini)

Gino Benotto, Conegliano, Treviso

(Yield: 4 servings)

¼ cup extra-virgin olive oil
½ leek
(diced, white and light green only)
1 onion (diced)
1 celery stalk (diced)
1 carrot (diced)
2 zucchini, green and yellow
(seeds removed, diced)
½ cup parsley (finely chopped)

¹/₈ teaspoon cinnamon
salt and freshly ground pepper
1 cup arborio rice
5½ cups water with 1 chicken bouillon cube
(or 5½ cups chicken stock) warmed
1 tablespoon butter
Parmigiano-Reggiano or Parmesan cheese
(grated)

1. Warm oil in large skillet over medium heat. Cook leeks, onions and celery until onions are translucent.

2. Add carrots, zucchini, parsley, cinnamon, salt and pepper; cook for another 2 minutes.

3. Add rice and cook until rice has been fully incorporated (approx. 2 to 3 more minutes).

4. Add enough heated broth to cover everything, stirring continuously.

5. Once the broth has been almost absorbed, add another ladle of broth and stir. Repeat until all broth has been used and the risotto has cooked for approx. 30 minutes.

6. When the risotto is al dente and creamy, remove pan from heat and re-season with salt and pepper.

7. Working quickly, add butter, and a good handful (to taste) of grated cheese. Stir until fully incorporated.

Serve immediately, topped with more cheese.

Vitello in Umido alla Bellunese
(Veal Stew)

Marisa Chemello, Cadola, Belluno

(Yield: 4 servings)

2 tablespoons extra-virgin olive oil
1 onion (diced)
2 pounds veal shoulder
(cut into large 1½-inch cubes)
1 rosemary sprig

5 garlic cloves (minced)
½ teaspoon freshly grated nutmeg
6 cups beef broth, warmed
(or 6 cups of water and 2 bouillon cubes)
1 tablespoon tomato paste
salt and freshly ground pepper

1. Warm oil in large Dutch oven or saucepan over medium heat and cook onions until translucent.
2. Add veal cubes and lightly brown on all sides (approx. 8 minutes).
3. Add rosemary, garlic and nutmeg. Mix well.
4. Add beef broth and tomato paste. Season with salt and pepper.
5. Once mixture has come to a boil, reduce to a simmer and cook covered for approx. 1 hour, stirring every 15 minutes.

Serve on top of polenta (page 308).

Fettuccine con Luganega, Funghi e Erbe Aromatiche
(Fettuccine, with Sausage, Mushrooms and Herbs)

Nereo Favrin, Loria, Treviso

(Yield: 4 servings)

1 pound fettuccine
3 tablespoons extra-virgin olive oil
1 pound (hot or mild) Italian sausage (see note)
1 tablespoon butter
1 cup chopped green onion
2 garlic cloves (minced)
2 cups sliced fresh button mushrooms

1 green pepper (diced)
1 cup parsley (finely chopped)
1 teaspoon fresh sweet basil
(4 medium leaves, finely chopped)
½ teaspoon (finely chopped) fresh oregano
¼ teaspoon (finely chopped) fresh rosemary
salt and freshly ground pepper

1. Bring large pot of salted water to a boil.

2. In large skillet over medium heat, add 1 tbsp oil and cook sausage for approx. 5 minutes, while waiting for water to boil.

3. Add pasta to boiling water after sausage has cooked.

4. Remove sausage from skillet and place on paper towels to drain grease.

5. In the same skillet, add remaining oil and butter and remaining ingredients and cook over medium heat. Stir until everything is incorporated (approx. 8 minutes).

6. Add sausage and cook for another 2 minutes.

7. Once the pasta is cooked al dente, drain and add to skillet. Mix thoroughly, seasoning with salt and pepper as required.

8. Remove skillet from heat and sprinkle with Parmesan cheese.

Serve immediately.

Note: when preparing the Italian sausage, remove and discard the casing and crumble the meat.

Pasta Carbonara

John Benotto, Conegliano, Treviso

(Yield: 4 servings)

1 pound bowties or rigatoni pasta
1/3 cup extra-virgin olive oil
1 onion (diced)
6 garlic cloves (minced)
1 pound pancetta or bacon
(cut into 1-inch squares)

1 egg
chili pepper flakes
(optional)
¾ cup grated Parmigiano-Reggiano cheese
(or Parmesan)
salt and freshly ground pepper

1. Bring large pot of salted water to a boil. Add pasta, giving it a good stir.

2. Warm oil in large Teflon-coated skillet over medium heat. Cook onions and garlic until onions are translucent.

3. Meanwhile, in another skillet over medium heat, cook the pancetta squares until slightly soft but not crisp (approx. 3 to 4 minutes).

4. Remove the pancetta (without the fat) from skillet and add to the onion/garlic mixture. Continue cooking for another 2 minutes.

5. By this time, your pasta should be cooked. Drain and add it to the skillet, giving it a good stir.

6. Add the egg. Mix thoroughly. Add chili pepper flakes and stir until everything is well mixed.

7. Remove from heat. Add the cheese and give it another stir. Season with salt and pepper to taste.

Serve hot and top with more cheese.

Coniglio alla Casalinga Bellunese
(Homestyle Rabbit)

Dario Chemello, Cadola, Belluno

(Yield: 4 servings)

1 rabbit
(about 3 lbs)
4 cups water (see note)
1 cup white vinegar (see note)

~

3 tablespoon extra-virgin olive oil
1 onion (diced)

1 rosemary sprig
1 teaspoon each salt and pepper
2 cups white wine
28 ounces tomato sauce (1 can)
water (enough to cover)
2 beef bullion cubes (broken)

1. Mix water and vinegar and thoroughly clean rabbit. Pat dry and cut into pieces.*

2. Warm oil in large skillet over medium heat. Brown rabbit on all sides (approx. 12 minutes).

3. Add onions and sauté until translucent.

4. Add rosemary, salt, pepper and wine. Allow the alcohol to evaporate.

5. Add tomato sauce and enough water to cover rabbit.

6. Add bullion cubes and mix well.

7. Once mixture has come to a boil, reduce heat to low and cook covered for approx. 1½ hours. Add more wine or water as needed so it does not dry out.

Serve with polenta (see page 308).

Note: the combination of 4 cups (1 litre) of water and 1 cup of vinegar is for cleaning wild rabbit. If you purchased the rabbit from a butcher it is probably clean and this process can be skipped.

Selvaggina alla Cacciatora
(Wild Game – Hunters Style)

John Benotto, Conegliano, Treviso

Although there are many recipes for a Cacciatore, you will be very impressed with this one because of its simplicity and flavour.

(Yield: 4 servings)

¼ cup extra-virgin olive oil
1 whole chicken, duck or pheasant, cut into pieces (leaving skin on)
1 onion (finely chopped)
1 celery stalk (diced)
1 carrot (diced)
½ green pepper (diced)

1 teaspoon each, salt and freshly ground pepper
1/8 teaspoon cinnamon
1 rosemary sprig
16 ounces stewed tomatoes
1 teaspoon tomato paste
6 ounces dry white wine
12 ounces water
1 teaspoon *pesto* (optional)

1. Warm half the oil in large skillet over medium heat until slightly smoking.
2. Brown chicken, duck or pheasant pieces on all sides and place pieces in a 9x13 oven casserole dish.
3. Add remaining oil to skillet and sauté all vegetables until tender (approx. 5 minutes).
4. Add salt, pepper, cinnamon, rosemary, stewed tomatoes, tomato paste, white wine and water. Add pesto if desired. Once it is boiling, lower heat to a simmer for 5 minutes.
5. While cooking vegetables, preheat oven to 350°F.
6. Pour vegetables into casserole dish to cover the meat.
7. Roast in oven, uncovered, for 1½ hours. Add more water or wine as necessary.

Traditionally served over polenta (page 308) or rice (page 306).

FRIULI-VENEZIA GIULIA

CAPITAL

Trieste

RED WINE

Refosco dal P.R.

WHITE WINE

Bianco Friulano or Ribolla Gialla

Finocchi in Pentola
(Fennel in a Pan)

Paolo Savio, Buia, Udine

(Yield: 4 servings)

2 tablespoons salted butter
1 large fennel bulb
(cut into 4 or more pieces)
1 teaspoon salt (or to taste)
1 teaspoon pepper (or to taste)
1 teaspoon tomato paste
½ cup water
Parmesan cheese

1. Melt butter in skillet over low heat. Add fennel pieces. Cook covered until they start to turn a light golden colour (approx. 5 minutes).

2. Combine salt, pepper, tomato paste and water in a small bowl. Mix.

3. Add mixture to the skillet and cook covered for approx. 3 minutes. Add water as needed.

Serve as a side dish with a little grated Parmesan cheese.

Melanzane alla Parmigiana
(Eggplant Parmesan)

Claudia Monte, Caneva, Pordenone

This recipe was handed down to me from my mother, Augusta Monte.

(Yield: 2 servings)

12 ounces crushed tomatoes
2 tablespoons tomato paste
½ cup extra-virgin olive oil
2 eggplants (large)

2 cups breadcrumbs
½ cup grated Parmesan cheese
½ cup parsley
(finely chopped)
salt and freshly ground pepper (to taste)
½ pound shredded Mozzarella cheese

1. Mix in a bowl tomatoes and tomato paste. Add 2 tablespoons olive oil and a pinch of salt and mix again.

2. Add tomato mixture to skillet over medium heat. Once it comes to a boil, lower heat to a simmer and cook for approx. 30 minutes. Set aside.

3. Cut eggplant crosswise into ½-inch slices. Place in bowl and cover with hot water. Allow to stand for approx. 5 minutes.

4. Drain and dry the slices with paper towels. Set aside.

5. Add remaining olive oil to another skillet and fry eggplant slices over high heat (approx. 3 minutes per side, or until soft and light brown). Remove from skillet and sprinkle with salt and pepper. Set aside.

6. Mix breadcrumbs, Parmesan cheese, parsley, salt and pepper (to taste) in a bowl. Set aside.

7. Place a layer of sliced eggplant on the bottom of a 6x6 baking dish. Sprinkle with breadcrumb mixture and add some of the tomato sauce mixture.

8. Continue building layers until all ingredients have been used.

9. Top with Mozzarella cheese and bake in oven preheated to 350°F for approx. 10 to 12 minutes, or until the Mozzarella turns slightly brown.

Allow to rest for 5 minutes and serve.

Insalata di Fagioli
(Bean Salad)

Marisa (Pez) Figgins, Beano Codroipo, Udine

(Yield: 4 servings)

28 ounces cooked Romano beans
(2 cans, drained and rinsed)
¼ onion (sliced thinly)
¼ cup parsley (finely chopped)
½ lemon juiced
(more if necessary)
2 tablespoon extra-virgin olive oil
salt and freshly ground pepper (to taste)

1. Combine beans, onion and parsley in a bowl and toss gently.
2. Add lemon juice and mix. Taste, adding more lemon juice as required.
3. Add oil, salt and pepper (to taste). Mix.

Serve as a cold side dish.

Crespe di Zucchine
(Zucchini Crepes)

Claudia Monte, Caneva, Pordenone

This recipe was handed down to me from my mother, Augusta Monte.

(Yield: 10 crepes)

3 cups grated zucchini
(coarse or fine)
1 egg
1 teaspoon salt
½ teaspoon black pepper

½ cup flour
1 teaspoon baking powder
extra-virgin olive oil
½ cup melted butter
grated Parmesan cheese

1. Combine zucchini, egg, salt and pepper in a bowl. Mix thoroughly. Sift flour and baking powder over the mixture and mix again.

2. Warm 1 tablespoon of oil in large skillet or griddle over medium heat.

3. Using a scoop or large spoon, drop a 3-inch disc onto the heated surface.

4. Cook until brown and then flip and cook other side (approx. 3 minutes each side). Continue adding oil as required.

Serve with melted butter and top with Parmesan cheese.

Insalata Tiepida di Lenticchie e Trota Salmonata
(Warm Lentils and Trout Salad)

Elisa (Savio) Piemonte, Buia, Udine

(Yield: 4 servings)

1½ cups dried lentils
1 lemon
(juiced and quartered)
1 red onion
12 cherry tomatoes

6 ounces San Daniel's salmon trout
½ cup toasted olives
½ cup roughly chopped basil
extra-virgin olive oil
salt and freshly ground pepper

1. Soak lentils in cold water for a few hours. Drain and put lentils in a saucepan with lemon juice and the quartered lemons. Cover with water and cook for 40 minutes over medium heat. Add 1 teaspoon salt at end.

2. In the meantime, cut onion into thin slices and arrange them on a plate. Sprinkle with salt and olive oil, then cover with plastic wrap and put the plate in the fridge until you are ready to serve.

3. Clean cherry tomatoes, keeping leafstalks attached. Place them in a baking dish. Sprinkle with oil and cover with aluminum foil. Bake in oven preheated to 200°F for 10-15 minutes.

4. Cut salmon trout into slices and reserve in the fridge until ready to serve.

5. Drain the lentils when cooked. Place them in a bowl.

6. Add the marinated onions and the cherry tomatoes, salmon trout, toasted olives and chopped basil.

7. Season with salt and pepper, sprinkle with 2 tablespoons of oil and gently mix.

Serve as an appetizer in a Martini glass.

Scaloppine di Patate
(Scalloped Potatoes)

Elisa (Piasentin) Zanotti, Morsano al Tagliamento, Pordenone

(Yield: 4 to 6 servings)

SAUCE:
1 can (10 ounces) condensed
cream of celery or mushroom soup
½ cup milk
¼ cup Italian parsley (chopped)
dash of black pepper

4 cups potatoes
(sliced thin, peel left on or off)
1 small onion (thinly sliced)
1 tablespoon butter (cold)
dash of paprika

1. Combine condensed soup, milk, parsley and pepper in a bowl. Set aside.

2. Using a greased 1½-quart casserole dish, arrange alternating layers of potatoes, onions and sauce mixture. Continue building layers until all of the potatoes and onions have been used.

3. Dot the top layer with bits of butter and sprinkle with paprika. Bake covered in oven preheated to 325°F for 1½ hours. Uncover and bake for another 15 minutes or until potatoes are done.

Options: add grated cheese, sliced mushrooms, diced green peppers or vegetables of your choice.

Risotto con Valeriana o Spinaci
(Risotto with Herbs)

Angelina Pez, Pozzuolo del Friuli, Udine

(Yield: 4 servings)

3½ tablespoons butter
1 onion (diced)
½ pound sculpit or spinach (chopped fine)
1½ cups arborio rice

½ cup dry white wine
6 cups of chicken or vegetable broth (warm)
Montasio cheese (grated)
salt and freshly ground pepper

1. Sauté onion in half of the butter in large skillet over medium heat until translucent.

2. Add sculpit (valerian) or spinach and stir, cooking for approx. 3 minutes.

3. Add rice and continue cooking until rice is opaque, (approx. 5 minutes).

4. Add wine and continue cooking until the alcohol has evaporated.

5. Add enough broth to cover rice and continue stirring until it comes to a boil. Lower heat to a simmer and continue to add broth a cup at a time.

6. Continue stirring and adding broth until rice is al dente (approx. 30 minutes).

7. When rice is cooked, remove from heat and add remaining butter and a lot of grated cheese (to taste).

Mix thoroughly and serve.

Rotolo di Pasta e Spinaci e Ricotta
(Pasta Rolls Stuffed with Spinach and Ricotta Cheese)

Lucia Costella, Pasiano di Prato, Pordenone

(Yield: 4 servings)

PASTA:

3 cups flour

2 whole eggs

2 tablespoons warm water

pinch of salt

FILLING:

1 pound spinach

(cleaned and roughly chopped)

pinch of salt

1 cup Ricotta cheese

1 cup Parmesan cheese (grated)

2 egg yolks

1/8 teaspoon ground nutmeg

SAUCE:

7 tablespoons butter

or tomato sauce

Parmesan cheese

1. **MAKE THE PASTA:** Sift flour onto a working surface and make a well in the centre. Add eggs, water and salt and slowly incorporate all the flour. Mix completely, then form a ball and knead until smooth. Wrap ball tightly with plastic wrap and allow to sit for approx. ½ hour.

2. **MAKE THE FILLING:** Cook spinach with 2 tablespoons of water and a pinch of salt in a skillet over medium heat for approx. 5 minutes (or until entirely wilted). Remove from heat, drain and wrap spinach in a clean towel and squeeze out excess liquid. Combine drained spinach, Ricotta and Parmesan cheese, egg yolks, and nutmeg in a bowl and set aside.

3. Remove the pasta dough, divide into 4 pieces and roll out each as thinly as possible on a flour surface.

4. Spread the filling evenly over the dough to within one inch of its edges. Roll up the dough into a cylinder and pinch the ends and seam to hold the filling in place.

5. Gently lower the rolls into a large pot of boiling water and cook for approx. 1 hour.

6. Remove and drain. Place onto serving dishes and top with melted butter or warm tomato sauce and garnish with grated Parmesan cheese.

Conchiglie Ricotta e Spinaci al Forno
(Baked Pasta Shells with Spinach Ricotta Filling)

Elisa (Piasentin) Zanotti, Morsano al Tagliamento, Pordenone

(Yield: 4 servings)

20 jumbo shells
FILLING:
1 pound fresh spinach
(10 ounces frozen chopped)
¼ cup water
¼ cup diced onion
2 tablespoons butter
1 egg (beaten)
²/3 cup Ricotta cheese

½ cup grated Parmesan cheese
1/8 teaspoon freshly ground nutmeg
SAUCE:
1 tablespoon butter
1 tablespoon finely diced onion
3 tablespoons all-purpose flour
2 cups milk
½ cup white wine
1 cup shredded Mozzarella (4 ounces)

1. Cook pasta in boiling salted water until tender (5 minutes), drain and rinse in cold water. Set aside.

MAKE THE FILLING:

2. Add spinach and water to a large skillet and cook covered for 3 to 5 minutes over medium heat. Drain well. Squeeze spinach to remove excess moisture. Chop fine and set aside.

3. In same skillet, over medium heat, sweat onions in butter until tender. Add chopped spinach and cook for approx. 3 minutes. Remove from heat and allow to cool.

4. After it has cooled, add the spinach mixture, egg, both cheeses and nutmeg in a bowl. Mix thoroughly.

5. Use 1 round tablespoon to fill each pasta shell. Arrange the shells in a greased 12x7 baking dish.

MAKE THE SAUCE:

6. In small saucepan over medium heat, cook onions in butter until translucent. Stir in flour and milk and continue stirring until it comes to a gentle boil. Lower heat to a simmer and add wine and Mozzarella cheese, stirring until incorporated.

7. Pour sauce over pasta shells and sprinkle with nutmeg. Cover dish with foil and bake in oven preheated to 350°F for 25 to 30 minutes.

Serve immediately.

Patate in Tecia
(Potato Salad)

Claudia Monte, Caneva, Pordenone

This recipe was handed down to me from my mother, Augusta Monte.

(Yield: 6 servings)

1½ pounds potatoes
4 tablespoons lard
1 onion (diced)
½ cup parsley (chopped)
1 cup white wine
1 cup chicken broth
salt and freshly ground pepper

1. Wash and scrub potatoes, leaving the skin on. Place potatoes in a large pot of salted water and boil until almost tender. Drain, peel, and set aside to cool, then slice into ½-inch thicknesses.

2. Melt lard in a large skillet over medium heat. Cook onions until translucent.

3. Add sliced potatoes, and using the back of a wooden spoon, break potatoes up into smaller pieces.

4. Add parsley, wine and broth and season with salt and pepper to taste. Allow to simmer for approx. 2 minutes or until potatoes start to turn golden but not dark.

Serve warm or at room temperature.

Spezzatino di Carne
(Beef Stew)

Rosina Bellina, Venzone, Udine

(Yield: 6 servings)

2 tablespoons butter
¼ cup extra-virgin olive oil
4 pounds beef
(cut into 1½-inch cubes)
1 cup water
4 beef or chicken bouillon cubes
1 onion (diced)
1 tablespoon finely chopped fresh rosemary

1 tablespoon finely chopped sage
1 tablespoon ground nutmeg
1 tablespoon ground cinnamon
3 garlic cloves (minced)
5 tablespoons finely chopped parsley
1½ cups red wine (or water)

1. Warm butter and oil in large Dutch oven over medium heat. Add beef and brown on all sides. Dilute bouillon cubes in water and add to beef.

2. Add remaining ingredients. Once mixture has come to a boil, lower heat to a simmer and cook for approx. 4 hours with the lid on, stirring often. After 2 hours add 1½ cups of red wine or water.

3. Check constantly to make sure there is liquid (do not allow to dry out), ensuring beef remains moist. Add more water (or wine) as necessary.

Serve with lots of crusty Italian bread.

Bocconcini di Pollo in Camicia
(Chicken Thighs Wrapped in Pancetta)

Gabriella Nadalin, Morsano al Tagliamento, Pordenone

(Yield: 4 servings)

12 chicken thighs (skin on)
12 pancetta or bacon strips
¾ cup flour
½ cup extra-virgin olive oil
3 tablespoons butter

1 garlic clove (minced)
¾ cup white wine
1 chicken bouillon cube
24 fresh sage leaves

1. Using a toothpick to hold it in place, wrap a strip of pancetta around each thigh. Dredge each thigh with flour and shake off excess. Set aside.

2. Warm oil and butter in large skillet over medium heat. Add garlic, wine and bouillon cube. Stir for approx. 1 minute.

3. Add thighs to skillet and cook for approx. 15 minutes. Turn over and continue cooking until they are slightly golden or fully cooked. Once cooked, remove thighs from skillet and set aside.

4. Reduce heat to low and add sage leaves to remaining mixture. Cook until slightly crisp, careful not to overcook, approx. 3 minutes.

5. Divide thighs evenly onto 4 plates and garnish with sage leaves.

Serve while warm.

Insalata di Riso
(Rice Salad)

Bruna (Zanotti) Pinard, Morsano al Tagliamento, Pordenone

(Yield: 4 servings)

1 cup rice
4 cooked Italian sausages
(finely diced)
7 ounces solid white tuna broken
into small pieces
4 ounces favourite cheese
(cut into ¼-inch)
4 ounces prosciutto cotto or cooked ham
(diced ¼-inch)

1 cup green olives, pits removed
(finely diced)
1 hard-boiled egg (diced ¼-inch)
1 tomato (diced ¼-inch)
½ green pepper (diced ¼-inch)
¾ cup mayonnaise
2 tablespoons fresh lemon juice
radicchio salad leaves
parsley for garnish

1. Cook rice as per instructions on page 306 and allow to cool to room temperature.

2. Mix rice, sausage, tuna, cheese, prosciutto cotto, olives, egg, tomato and pepper in a large bowl and place in fridge until ready to serve.

3. When ready to serve, add mayonnaise and lemon juice and mix thoroughly.

4. Layer a plate with large radicchio leaves and place rice mixture onto leaves. Garnish with a few sprigs of parsley.

Asparagi Marinati e Prosciutto
(Marinated Asparagus and Prosciutto)

Marcellina Bortolin, Porcia, Pordenone

Adapting this recipe from the traditional and simple Friuliano method, my mother Marcellina usually prepared boiled vegetables by sprinkling them with salt and pepper and drizzling them with oil and wine vinegar to taste. —Elena Petruzzi

(Yield: 8 servings)

2 pounds fresh asparagus
(cleaned and trimmed)
MARINADE:
½ cup extra-virgin olive oil
¼ cup white wine vinegar or rice wine vinegar
(or to taste)

2 tablespoons Dijon mustard
2 tablespoons honey
2 teaspoons dried tarragon
(or thyme)

¼ pound prosciutto (thinly sliced)

1. Place asparagus in saucepan with small amount of boiling water and cook for approx. 4 minutes, or until tender. Remove asparagus and plunge into ice-cold water to stop cooking process. Dry, then place asparagus in shallow baking dish.

2. While asparagus is cooking, combine oil, wine vinegar, Dijon Mustard, honey and tarragon (or thyme) in a jar. Cover tightly and shake vigorously.

Pour dressing over asparagus, cover and allow to chill, marinating for 2 hours.

3. When ready to serve, remove asparagus from dressing, arrange on a platter topped with prosciutto and drizzle with a little of the marinade.

For a creamier dressing use a blender. Crisp a few pieces of the pancetta and sprinkle on top.

Spinaci in Casseruola
(Spinach Casserole)

Augusta (Bortolotto) Quagliotto, Fiume Veneto, Pordenone

(Yield: 4 servings)

1½ pounds fresh spinach
(chopped rough)
4 eggs (beaten)
1 onion (diced)
½ cup butter (melted)

½ cup grated Parmesan cheese
¼ teaspoon pepper
¼ teaspoon garlic powder
½ teaspoon Italian seasoning

1. In large saucepan of salted boiling water, cook spinach until wilted (approx. 5 minutes). Drain and run cold water over spinach to cool it and stop cooking process. Once cooled, squeeze out as much liquid as possible and give spinach another rough chop.

2. Combine spinach and eggs in bowl and mix thoroughly. Add remaining ingredients and mix again.

3. Grease an oven baking dish and sprinkle some Parmesan cheese over dish. Add spinach mixture and sprinkle more cheese on the top.

4. Bake in oven preheated to 350°F for approx. 35 to 40 minutes. Remove from oven and allow to sit for 10 minutes before serving.

Serve warm or at room temperature.

Umido alla Regina
(Regina's Homemade Stew)

Regina (Facchin) Moro, Tramonti di Sopra, Pordenone

(Yield: 15-20 servings)

1 pound veal (cut into 2-inch cubes)

1 pound pork stew (cut into 2-inch cubes)

2 pounds boneless chicken thighs
(cut into 2-inch cubes)

1 pound Italian sausage
(cut into 2-inch lengths)

2 pounds baby back ribs
(cut into 2 ribs per strip)

10 medium potatoes
(cut in half)

MARINADE:

2 tablespoons garlic powder

Italian spices (to your liking)

4 tablespoons extra-virgin olive oil

2 tablespoons each salt and pepper

SAUCE:

8 tablespoons extra-virgin olive oil

2 tablespoons butter

2 large carrots (diced)

3 celery stalks (diced)

½ whole garlic head (minced)

2 large onions (diced)

1 cup parsley
(finely chopped)

1 rosemary sprig
(roughly chopped)

10 ounces white wine

Italian spices (to your liking)

28 ounces diced canned tomatoes with herbs and
spices

5½ ounces tomato paste with herbs and spices

4 bay leaves

2 vegetable bouillon cubes

1. Place all meats in large bowl or ziplock freezer bag. Place potatoes in another.

2. Mix ingredients for marinade and add half of marinade to each bag or bowl. Mix well. Place in fridge and allow to marinate for approx. 1 hour. If marinating overnight, toss every few hours; otherwise toss every 30 minutes.

3. Warm 4 tablespoons of olive oil in a very large saucepan or large pot over medium-high heat. Braise all meats until seared and sealed (10 to 15 minutes). Add potatoes and do the same for approx. 10 minutes.

4. Meanwhile, heat 4 tablespoons of oil and butter in another large saucepan over medium heat. Add carrots, celery, garlic, onions, parsley, rosemary, white wine, and Italian spices to taste. Sauté until onions are translucent and wine has been absorbed (approx. 15 minutes). Add diced tomatoes, paste, bay leaves and bouillon cubes and stir well.

5. Once mixture has come to a boil, turn heat down to a simmer and cook for approx. 30 minutes.

6. Add braised meats and potatoes to sauce and allow mixture to cook over low heat (a simmer) for approx. 1½ hours.

Serve immediately.

Umido
(Polenta Lasagna)

Rick Tonial, Sesto al Reghena, Pordenone

This is an old northern Italian recipe, commonly known as Umido. It was made with scrap pieces of various meats, and served on a bed of polenta. This recipe is a result of my father's (Bruno Tonial) influence on me as a cook. My Dad always cooked our Sunday meals and he had a passion to create flavourful dishes.

(Yield: 8 servings)

1 pound Italian sausage
(cut in 1-inch pieces)
2 pounds stewing veal (cubed)
1 pound stewing beef (cubed)
1 slab pork ribs
(dressed and cut between each bone)
4 ¼-inch slices pancetta (diced)
extra-virgin olive oil
1 teaspoon each dried, thyme, oregano,
basil, sage, rosemary
1 onion (diced)
1 garlic head (peeled and minced)
1 celery stalk (diced)
1 carrot (diced)
8 ounces tomato paste
1 bottle white wine
2 cups chicken broth
3 pounds (48 ounces) San Marzano tomatoes
(puréed through a passatutto)
1 chicken bouillon cube
1 teaspoon cinnamon
salt and freshly ground pepper
4 bay leaves
4 cups medium-grain polenta
16 cups water
4 cups Parmesan cheese
6 cups shredded Mozzarella cheese

1. Place all meats and pancetta in large bowl, drizzle with olive oil, and sprinkle with ½ teaspoon (each) of thyme, oregano, basil, sage, rosemary, salt and pepper. Toss. Spread onto a large cookie sheet and roast in oven preheated to 400°F for approx. 40 minutes, mixing occasionally until meat has caramelized but is not completely cooked.
2. Warm ½ cup of extra-virgin olive oil in large oven-ready saucepan over medium heat. Sauté onions, garlic, celery, and carrots until onions are translucent.
3. Increase heat to high and add tomato paste, cooking for approx. 8 minutes or until colour gets darker. Add semi-cooked meats with 2 cups of white wine. Allow mixture to boil for 10 minutes, then add chicken broth and tomatoes. Deglaze the cookie sheet (used to cook the meat) with some wine or water and add this liquid mixture to the saucepan with meat.
4. Add chicken bouillon, ½ teaspoon each of thyme, oregano, basil, sage and rosemary, 1 teaspoon of cinnamon and 4 bay leaves. Re-season with salt and pepper to taste. Once mixture has come to a boil cover and place in oven preheated to 350°F for 4 hours, stirring hourly.
5. Meanwhile, make polenta (as per instructions on page 308).
6. On pre-greased cookie pans, pour the hot polenta and spread to approx. ¼-inch thick. Place pans in fridge, and cool polenta for a least an hour. Then cut into lasagna-sized strips.
7. Remove meat from pot. Let meat cool and then remove all bones, shredding the meat (like pulled pork). Return meat back to pot containing the rich tomato sauce.
8. Using a 9x13 oven dish, ladle some of the meat sauce on the bottom. Cover with a layer of polenta strips, cover these with meat sauce, and sprinkle with Parmesan and Mozzarella cheese. Continue building your layers until all ingredients have been used, ending with the meat sauce on top.
9. Cover with aluminum foil and bake in oven preheated to 350°F for approx. 1 hour. Remove and allow it to sit for 10 minutes. Serve.

The key to the sauce is the rich layers of flavours that are created by caramelizing the meats. The baking of the Umido for 4 hours results in a rich tomato sauce.

LOMBARDIA

CAPITAL
Milano

RED WINE
Inferno (Valtellina Superiore)

WHITE WINE
Lugana

Polenta Concia
(Polenta with Two Cheeses)

Elisabetta (Mossini) Lia, Ardenno, Sondrio

(Yield: 6 servings)

1 pound yellow cornmeal

8 cups milk

salt

½ pound Fontina cheese (diced)

¼ pound Gruviera cheese
or Swiss cheese (diced)

½ pound butter

1 teaspoon ground sage

1. Cook polenta in milk (see instructions to make polenta on page 308) for 30 minutes.

2. Add Fontina and Gruviera and continue cooking until well-blended.

3. Pour onto plate or in bowl to form. Add melted butter infused with sage.

Serve in the soft state with your favourite sauce or after it has completely cooled and been cut into wedges.

Risotto alla Milanese
(Risotto with Saffron)

Nives Rossi, Milano

(Yield: 6 servings)

4 cups chicken broth (hot)

2 sachets saffron

3 tablespoons butter

1 onion (diced)

2 cups arborio rice

1½ cups white wine

salt and freshly ground pepper

½ cup grated Parmesan cheese

1. Warm broth in saucepan over medium heat. Add saffron. Once boiling, reduce to simmer and keep warm (the broth will turn a yellow colour).

2. Melt butter in large skillet over medium heat and sauté onions until translucent. Add rice and stir well until all grains are coated with butter.

3. Raise heat to medium-high. Add wine, salt and pepper to taste; continue stirring until wine is absorbed by rice.

4. Lower heat to medium and add enough broth to cover rice. Continue stirring. Add broth a cup at a time until absorbed (approx. 30 minutes).

5. When rice is cooked and creamy, remove from heat, add cheese, and mix thoroughly.

6. Cover and allow risotto to sit for approx. 5 minutes.

Serve on individual plates or bowls and top with extra cheese.

Pesce in Carpione
(Cod in Wine/Vinegar Sauce)

Rita (Corti) Ostinelli, Erba, Como

(Yield: 4 servings)

1 pound codfish or trout fillets
white flour (for dredging)
2 tablespoons extra-virgin olive oil
2 onions (sliced)
8 ounces white wine
1 cup white vinegar
salt and freshly ground pepper
1/8 cup parsley (finely chopped)

1. Dredge fillets in flour and set aside.
2. Warm oil in large skillet over medium heat and sauté onions.
3. Add wine and vinegar. Cook for another minute and stir well.
4. Reduce heat to low and add fillets, salt, and pepper. Cook covered for approx. 15 to 20 minutes.
5. Garnish with parsley.

Serve the fish on a platter, covered with onions and sauce from the pan, and sprinkled with parsley. This can also be refrigerated up to 3 days and served at room temperature.

Bruscitt
(Beef Strips in Wine)

Luciano Corti, Erba, Como

This is a recipe that my father loved making and we all enjoyed. —Rita

3½ tablespoons butter
2 bay leaves
1 garlic clove (minced)
1½ pounds tender beef meat
(cut into 1-inch strips)

2 ounces pancetta
(diced)
2 cups red wine
salt and freshly ground pepper

1. Melt butter in large skillet over medium heat. Add bay leaves and garlic; cook until fragrant (approx. 1 minute).

2. Add meat strips and pancetta. Mix well until all is coated with butter. Cook covered for 15 minutes over low heat, stirring occasionally.

3. Add wine and increase heat to medium-high until boiling. Return heat to low and continue cooking until wine is reduced by half. Discard bay leaves.

Season with salt and pepper and serve immediately.

Great served by itself or with a side dish of polenta (page 308).

Cotolette alla Milanese
(Veal Cutlets)

Nives Rossi, Milano

(Yield: 4 servings)

6 veal cutlets
(can be substituted with pork)
salt and freshly ground pepper
½ cup flour
2 eggs
1 cup breadcrumbs

½ cup grated Parmesan cheese
½ teaspoon ground nutmeg
½ cup extra-virgin olive oil
3 tablespoons butter
½ lemon cut into slices

1. Using a meat mallet, pound cutlets to ¼-inch thickness. Season with salt and pepper.

2. Sift flour onto plate. In bowl beat eggs. On another plate mix breadcrumbs, cheese and nutmeg.

3. Take each cutlet and dredge first in flour, then egg, and finally in breadcrumb mixture. Set aside.

4. In large skillet over medium heat, melt butter with oil and fry cutlets on each side for approx. 2 minutes or until cooked and golden. Move cutlets to paper-lined plate to remove excess oil.

Re-season with salt and pepper and serve with lemon slices.

Cassoeüla/Bottagio
(Stewed Pork with Savoy Cabbage)

Marina (Padovan) Lia, Como

(Yield: 4 servings)

3½ tablespoons butter

1 onion (diced)

2 ounces pancetta (diced)

1 pound pork ribs
(cut into 2-inch pieces)

1 pork foot
(cubed 1-inch pieces)

1 pound pork cheeks
(cut into 1-inch pieces)

2 carrots (diced)

3 tomatoes (diced)

1 celery stalk (diced)

1 savoy cabbage head (sliced thin)

salt and freshly ground pepper

1 pound pork sausages
(cut into 2-inch pieces)

3 cups vegetable broth

1. Melt butter in large saucepan or Dutch oven over medium heat and cook onions with pancetta until onions are golden.

2. Add pork meats (except sausage). Cook for approx. 5 minutes.

3. Add carrots, tomatoes and celery. Continue cooking for approx. 10 minutes. Add cabbage and season with salt and pepper. Cook until cabbage has wilted.

4. Add sausage and enough broth to cover. Bring to boil and then reduce to simmer.

5. Cook for approx. 2 hours, stirring occasionally and adding water or broth as needed. *Serve with polenta (page 308).*

Risotto con Pesce Persico
(Risotto with Perch)

Aurelia (Capraro) Di Salvo, Como

(Yield: 4 servings)

5 tablespoons butter
1 small onion (diced)
1½ cups carnaroli rice
½ cup white wine
5 cups vegetable broth (hot)

1 pound perch fillets
flour (for dredging)
12 sage leaves
salt and freshly ground pepper

1. In large skillet over medium heat, cook onions in 2 tablespoons butter until translucent. Add rice and toast for a few minutes, stirring constantly. Add wine and continue stirring until wine has evaporated.

2. Reduce heat to simmer and add enough broth to cover rice; continue stirring until broth has been completely absorbed. Continue adding broth one ladle at a time, until rice is cooked al dente (approx. 30 minutes). Season with salt and pepper, remove from heat and cover to keep warm.

3. Dredge perch fillets in flour and shake off excess. Set aside.

4. While cooking risotto, in another skillet over medium heat melt remaining butter and fry perch fillets until golden, approx. 3-4 minutes per side. Remove fillets from skillet and set aside.

5. In same skillet, add sage leaves and cook until crisp but not brown. Add sage to risotto and mix well.

6. Transfer the risotto to 4 warm serving plates and top with perch fillets.

Serve immediately.

Pizzoccheri
(Buckwheat Flour Pasta)

Elisabetta (Mossini) Lia, Ardenno, Sondrio

(Yield: 4 servings)

3 cups buckwheat flour
½ cup water
white flour (for dusting)
½ pound potatoes (1-inch cubes)
½ cup finely sliced Swiss chard
½ cup finely sliced Savoy cabbage

½ cup butter
4 garlic cloves (minced)
10 sage leaves
salt and freshly ground pepper
2 ounces Gorgonzola cheese
(optional)

1. To make the pizzoccheri, in a bowl add flour and mix in water a little at a time until dough-like. Flatten into a disc. Lightly flour counter and roll dough to 1/8-inch thickness. Cut dough into ½-inch bands; cut bands into 2- or 3-inch pieces.

2. In pot of salted boiling water add potatoes and cook for approx. 5 minutes. Add Swiss chard and savoy cabbage to pot and cook for another 10 minutes. Add pizzoccheri and cook 6 to 7 minutes more.

3. With slotted spoon remove contents of pot and place in colander. Allow to drain and set aside.

4. Melt butter in large skillet over low heat. Sauté garlic and sage leaves (3 to 4 minutes). Add the pizzoccheri and vegetables to skillet, mixing all till coated.

5. Remove from heat, season with salt and pepper and top with cheese (optional).

Serve immediately.

Nervitt con L'Erbasalvia
(Calf's Nerves with Sage)

Aurelia (Capraro)Di Salvo, Como

(Yield: 4 servings)

2 calf feet
8 cups water
1 carrot (diced)
1 celery stalk (diced)
1 onion (diced)
bouquet of herbs
(thyme, rosemary, bay leaf)

3½ tablespoons butter
1 cup white beans (cooked)
10 sage leaves
3 tablespoons heavy cream
freshly grated nutmeg
salt and freshly ground pepper
grated Parmesan cheese

1. Put calf feet in large pot of salted water (8 cups), add carrot, celery, and onion, bouquet of herbs and salt. Allow to boil covered for 4 hours.

2. When feet are well-cooked remove and allow to cool. Separate the nerves, cut into pieces, and set aside.

3. Using a fine strainer, strain cooking liquid and reserve.

4. In saucepan over medium heat, add 4 cups of reserved liquid, and then add beans and sage. Cook for 5 to 7 minutes. Add heavy cream and pinch of nutmeg; stir well. Cook for 2 minutes. Add reserved nerves and cook for another minute. Remove from heat. Season with salt and pepper and a sprinkling of grated cheese.

Serve hot as an antipasto.

Paradello
(Apple Omelette)

Luciano Di Salvo, Como

(Yield: 6 servings)

5 eggs	1 cup milk
3 tablespoons sugar	1 apple
1 cup flour	(peeled, cored and diced fine)
1 teaspoon salt	2 tablespoons salted butter

1. In bowl, beat eggs with sugar until mixture is foamy.

2. Add flour, salt, milk and apples and combine thoroughly.

3. In 10-inch skillet over medium heat, melt butter and add mixture slowly so it completely covers bottom (like a large pancake). Cook for about 5 minutes and then flip. Cook other side for an additional 5 minutes or until lightly golden.

Serve as an appetizer.

PIEMONTE

CAPITAL

Torino

RED WINE

Barolo or Barbaresco

WHITE WINE

Asti Spumante (Moscato d'Asti)

Uova Ripiene con Acciughe
(Stuffed Eggs with Anchovies)

Giuseppina (Molinaro) Guelfo, Montanaro, Torino

(Yield: 4 servings)

4 eggs (1 for each person)
8 anchovies (mashed)
1 tablespoon butter (at room temperature)

1. Place eggs in saucepan and cover with 1 to 2 inches of cold water and bring to boil. Once boiling, turn off heat, cover pot, and allow to rest for about 15 minutes.

2. Remove eggs from pot and place in a bowl of cold water until cool enough to handle.

3. Peel eggs, cut each in half lengthwise, and remove yolks.

4. In a bowl mix yolks, anchovies and butter until creamy.

5. Stuff egg-white halves with mixture and serve as an appetizer, warm or at room temperature.

Acciughe al Verde
(Anchovy, Garlic, Parsley, Chili Spread)

Milena Gassino, Mazzè, Torino

Adding more garlic and chilies gives this spread a nice kick, as long as your neighbour is enjoying it with you!

(Yield: 4 servings)

½ pound fresh anchovies
(bones removed)
1 tablespoon wine vinegar
5 garlic cloves or more (minced)

1 bunch of parsley (finely chopped)
1 red hot chili pepper
2 tablespoons breadcrumbs
1 cup extra-virgin olive oil

1. Run anchovies under water to remove some salt. Pat dry.

2. Add vinegar, garlic, parsley, chili pepper, breadcrumbs and olive oil to blender. Blend well.

3. Add 2 or 3 anchovies and continue blending until you get a heavy cream mixture.

4. Lay remaining anchovies on serving dish and cover with mixture. Wrap with plastic film and allow to sit in fridge overnight.

5. When ready to serve, put a few anchovies on each dish, along with toasted Italian bread spread with leftover mixture.

Pinzimonio Ortaggi
(Italian Raw Vegetable Antipasto)

Andrea Guelfo, Ivrea, Torino

This is a beautiful and colourful appetizer.

(Yield: 4 servings)

2 celery stalks
(cut 3 inches long)
1 fennel bulb (quartered)
1 each sweet red and yellow peppers
(cleaned, cut 3 inches long)
2 carrots (peeled, cut ½ inch wide
and approx. 3 inches long)
1 radicchio head (quartered)

8 radishes (quartered)
lettuce
DIP:
½ cup extra-virgin olive oil
1 lemon (juiced)
1 teaspoon red or white wine vinegar
salt and freshly ground pepper

1. Once you have cleaned, sliced awnd chopped all vegetables, place them on a bed of lettuce next to small bowl that will contain dip.

2. In bowl, mix olive oil, lemon juice and vinegar. Season with salt and pepper.

3. Amounts for dip mixture are to your personal taste. Continue tasting until the combination is perfect.

Fonduta Piemontese
(Piedmont Cheese Fondue)

Giuseppe Moretti, Torino

Fontina is an Italian cheese made with cow's milk. Fontina cheese has been made in the Aosta Valley in the Alps since the 12th century. Although the version from Aosta is the original and the most famous, Fontina production occurs in other parts of Italy, such as Piedmont. Italian Fontina is fairly pungent and has an intense flavour; Fontina cheeses produced in other countries can be much milder. Young Fontina has a softer texture that is suitable for fondue.

(Yield: 4 servings)

1 pound Fontina cheese (diced/sliced)
1 cup milk
2 tablespoons butter

4 egg yolks
white truffle
black pepper

1. In a bowl combine Fontina cheese and milk and allow to sit in fridge, covered, for 2 hours.

2. Fill bottom of double boiler with water and set to medium heat.

3. When water boils, set upper pan in place and add butter, Fontina/milk mixture and egg yolks.

4. As contents start to melt, whisk until all ingredients have been incorporated (approx. 10 minutes).

5. Transfer to fondue pot; add either grated white truffle or freshly grated black pepper.

Serve with toasted Italian bread.

Minestra di Noci
(Walnut Soup)

Elena Ferrero, Novara

In Piedmont, where the walnut groves are abundant, walnut soup is normally made in the winter months.

(Yield: 4 servings)

1 pound shelled walnuts
1 cup milk
1 cup cream (half and half)

7 cups beef broth
sliced, crusted bread (day-old)
salt and freshly ground pepper (to taste)

1. In boiling saucepan of salted water, blanch walnuts for a few minutes. Drain and peel away walnut skins. If some skins remain do not worry; it will add a little extra colour to the soup.

2. In blender, purée all but ½ cup of walnuts with milk and cream. Mixture should be smooth and creamy. Set aside.

3. Boil broth in saucepan over medium heat. Once boiling, slowly pour in walnut-cream mixture, stirring constantly. Simmer for approx. 15 minutes. Serve hot. Season with salt and pepper.

4. Top each bowl with small amount of reserved chopped walnuts.

Serve this historical soup with buttered, hot crusty bread.

La Bagna Caoda
(Anchovy and Garlic Dip)

Adelina (Cernusco) Guelfo, Ivrea, Torino

(Yield: 4 servings)

8 anchovies
8 garlic cloves
½ cup extra-virgin olive oil
4 tablespoons butter
(at room temperature)
milk
salt and freshly ground pepper
Assorted vegetables such as: thistles, sweet peppers (fresh or roasted), Jerusalem artichokes,
white or red cabbage, endive, leek, fresh turnip, pumpkin slices (roasted or fried) hot
polenta slices (page 308) (cut into 3-inch bite-sized pieces).

1. Clean anchovies and remove bones.

2. In blender add anchovies, garlic, oil and butter and blend until creamy. Add more oil if necessary.

3. In saucepan on very low heat, add mixture and cook for approx. 5 minutes.

4. Add just enough milk to slightly cover mixture and continue stirring and cooking for another 10 minutes.

5. Season with salt and pepper.

Transfer the sauce into a fondue pot and keep warm when served.

Vitel Tonné
(Cold Braised Veal)

Rosalia Basano, Torino

Although the name of this recipe does not sound Italian, it is a true Italian dish whose origin has been disputed from North to South. Best served cold on a hot day.

(Yield: 10 servings)

2 pounds circle veal
(eye of round)
MARINADE:
2 tablespoons white vinegar
4 cups water
1 onion (diced)
3 cloves
5 peppercorns
1 small cinnamon stick

4 bay leaves
1 tablespoon of salt
2 tablespoons vegetable oil
1 cup beef broth

3 tablespoons butter
10 anchovies in salt
3 hard-boiled eggs (crumbled)
10 capers in salt

1. Place veal in large bowl and add vinegar, water, onions, cloves, peppercorns, cinnamon stick, bay leaves and 1 tablespoon of salt; cover and allow to marinate overnight in refrigerator, turning occasionally.

2. Remove veal and strain, reserving all liquid.

3. Warm oil in large oven-proof skillet over medium-high heat; sear veal until it has formed a nice crust all around. Add beef broth to skillet and place in oven preheated to 400°F. Roast for 15 to 20 minutes, turning occasionally.

4. Once cooked, remove from pan and allow to cool.

5. Meanwhile, using same skillet over medium heat, melt butter and cook anchovies for 2 minutes. Add eggs and reserved liquid and reduce heat to simmer.

6. Cook slowly and stir until heavy and cream-like (approx. 10 minutes).

7. Remove from heat, pour sauce into blender, and purée.

8. Plate the veal and top with sauce.

Serve at room temperature. Garnish with capers.

Vin Brulé
(Mulled Wine)

Giuseppe Guelfo, Montanaro, Torino

This is a traditional drink served during the winter months, especially around the Christmas holidays. Usually made using full-bodied wine.

(Yield: 1 serving)

2 cups dry red wine
1 cup sugar
2½ teaspoons ground cinnamon
4 cloves
1 lemon (cut into wedges)
pinch black pepper

Using a small saucepan, add all ingredients and bring to a boil
for approx. 7 minutes.

Serve with a wedge of lemon and a cinnamon stick while still warm.

Zucchine in Carpione
(Fried, Marinated Zucchini)

Adelina Cernusco, Ivrea, Torino

Carpione: this is an historical way in Piedmont to prepare zucchini, fish, chicken, breaded meat, eggs and any kind of food that will match the strong flavour of vinegar. The main ingredient is fried, and then marinated in vinegar and wine.

(Yield: 4 servings)

1 pound medium-sized zucchini
flour (for dredging)
3 tablespoons canola oil
MARINADE:
3 garlic cloves (minced)
1 onion (diced)

3 bay leaves
1 cup white or red wine vinegar
½ cup red wine
3 small sage branches (approx. 15 leaves)
salt and black pepper

1. Wash zucchini and slice lengthwise to ¼-inch thicknesses. Dredge zucchini slices in flour and shake off excess.

2. Warm oil in large skillet over medium heat and fry zucchini slices for approx. 1 minute per side. Place on paper towels to remove excess oil.

3. In same skillet, over medium heat, add garlic, onions and bay leaves. Cook until onions are translucent.

4. Add vinegar and cook for approx. 2 minutes more. Add wine and sage leaves and cook over high heat for 3 to 4 minutes.

5. Remove and discard bay leaves.

6. Arrange zucchini in layers in a dish, cover with marinade sauce, and allow to marinate 5 to 6 hours in refrigerator (or even better overnight). Season with salt and pepper to taste.

Involtini di Cavolo Verza
(Swiss Chard Pork Rolls)

Maria (Molinaro) Andreutti, Torino

(Yield: 4 servings)

3 slices stale white bread
¼ cup milk (more if needed)
1 pound pork sausage (skin removed)
1 large Swiss chard head (leaves separated)
3 tablespoons grated Parmesan cheese

4 teaspoons finely chopped fresh thyme
1 egg
8 tablespoons butter
salt and freshly ground pepper

1. Place bread in bowl and cover with milk. Allow soaking and softening. Once soft, squeeze as much milk out as possible and set aside.

2. Warm large skillet over medium heat. Cook and crumble pork sausage meat. Once fully cooked, remove meat, set aside and discard grease.

3. Bring saucepan of salted water to boil and blanch chard leaves for 1 to 2 minutes. Remove with slotted spoon and layer on paper towels. Remove as much water as possible and cover with paper towels.

4. In bowl add pork, Parmesan cheese, thyme, egg and bread mixture. Combine until smooth.

5. Take a Swiss chard leaf, place 1 tablespoon of mixture at end, and roll one full turn.

6. Fold sides of chard leaf inwards and continue rolling, using a toothpick to secure.

7. Warm large saucepan over medium heat and melt butter.

8. Add as many rolls as will fit and cook for 12 to 15 minutes.

Season with salt and pepper prior to serving.

Zuppa di Pane
(Bread Soup)

Laura Cena, Ivrea, Torino

Although the name suggests this is a soup, it's not. Zuppa di Pane originated as a poor man's dish, and though simple to make, it is very tasty; the process of experimenting with your own additions can be endless.

(Yield: 4 servings)

1 pound stale bread
1½ cups butter
1½ cups grated Parmesan cheese

4 cups chicken broth (warmed)
salt and freshly ground pepper

1. Slice bread to ¾-inch thicknesses and toast lightly.

2. Melt butter in small saucepan over medium heat, making sure it does not boil. Once melted remove from heat immediately.

3. Using 4 individual oven bowls, insert a layer of toasted bread, pour in some butter, and cover with cheese. Add second layer of bread, butter and cheese.

4. Fill each bowl with broth and cover with a final layer of Parmesan.

5. Place on middle rack of an oven preheated to 350°F and cook for approx. 20 minutes, or until tops are slightly browned.

Serve hot, season with salt and freshly ground pepper and add another sprinkling of cheese.

You can add Savoy cabbage, Swiss chard, etc. between two layers of bread.

VALLE D'AOSTA

CAPITAL
Aosta

RED WINE
Gamay

WHITE WINE
Blanc de Morgex et de La Salle

Costolette di Vitello alla Valdostana
(Veal Cutlets with Fontina Cheese and Truffles)

Mauro Pellisier, Villeneuve, Aosta

Fontina cheese and Valle d'Aosta are synonymous. The origin of the name itself is debated – does it refer to Mont Fontin or the Italian verb *fondere*, meaning "to melt?" – but either way, this cheese is one of the most outstanding of the area.

(Yield: 4 servings)

8 veal cutlets
1 white truffle (if available)
¼ pound Fontina cheese
salt and freshly ground pepper

flour (for dredging)
2 eggs
breadcrumbs (for coating)
6 tablespoons butter

1. Laying each cutlet flat, pierce side opposite bone with sharp knife to create a pocket-like incision.

2. Cut truffle and cheese into thin pieces and insert into cut pockets, ensuring incision can be closed with a toothpick.

3. Season cutlets with salt and pepper. Dredge them in flour, shaking off excess.

4. In bowl beat eggs and add a pinch of pepper. Dip cutlets into egg mixture.

5. Roll cutlets in breadcrumbs, making sure all sides are coated.

6. Melt butter in large skillet over medium-high heat. Cook cutlets until golden on both sides, flipping every 5 to 8 minutes.

Serve while hot.

If white truffles are not available, garlic slivers can be used, giving it a different and wonderful flavour. Try it both ways.

Zuppa Paysanne
(The Peasant's Rich Soup)

Bruno Franchino, Arvier, Aosta

(Yield: 4 servings)

1 loaf day-old Italian bread
¼ pound Fontina cheese (8 to 10 thin slices)
¼ pound Toma cheese (8 to 10 thin slices)
½ cup grated Parmigiano cheese
4 cups chicken or beef broth (warm)

1. Cut the bread into ¾-inch slices.
2. Using a 9x12 baking dish, alternate layers of bread and Fontina/Toma cheese. Sprinkle Parmigiano on top.
3. Pour warm broth over dish and bake in oven preheated to 350°F for approx. 10 minutes.

Serve immediately with some of the broth.

Alternatively, you can use 4 individual oven bowls. Layer as above.

Tagliatelle Funghi e Noci
(Tagliatelle with Mushrooms and Walnuts)

Mario Franchino, Leverogne, Aosta

(Yield: 4 servings)

1 pound tagliatelle
½ cup dried mushrooms (preferably Porcini)
3½ tablespoons butter
2 onions (diced)
2 tablespoons finely chopped (Italian parsley)

1 cup Marsala wine
¼ cup cream
salt and freshly ground pepper
½ cup chopped walnuts
grated Parmigiano cheese

1. Soak dry mushrooms in warm water until soft.

2. Melt half of butter in skillet over medium heat; add onions and parsley. Sauté until onions are translucent.

3. Drain. Add mushrooms and Marsala. Reduce heat to low and cook covered for approx. 20 minutes.

4. In the meantime bring pot of salted water to boil. Halfway through cooking time for mushrooms, add pasta to water.

5. When mushrooms are cooked, add remaining butter, cream, salt and pepper (to taste). Cook for another 2 minutes.

6. Remove from heat, add chopped walnuts. Mix well.

7. When the tagliatelle is al dente, drain and add to skillet. Add grated Parmigiano, toss well and serve immediately.

Gnocchi di Zucca
(Pumpkin Gnocchi)

Silvana (Perrier) Franchino, Valgrisenche, Aosta

(Yield: 4 servings)

3 pounds pumpkin (whole or 24 ounces canned)
1 tablespoon extra-virgin olive oil
4 tablespoons flour (00 type)
½ cup grated Parmigiano cheese
2 eggs

salt and freshly ground pepper
½ cup butter (melted)
3 tablespoons finely chopped sage
3 ounces Fontina cheese (diced)

1. Cut pumpkin into big slices. Discard seeds or save to roast. Brush slices with oil and bake in oven preheated to 350°F until tender.

2. Scoop out pumpkin meat and mash in bowl.

3. Once cooled, add flour, Parmigiano, eggs, and a pinch of salt and pepper. Mix well.

4. Scoop out a teaspoon of the mixture, rolling it in an oval shape. Set on a lightly floured cookie sheet.

5. Bring pot of salted water to boil and add gnocchi. Once they rise to surface remove with slotted spoon and set aside.

6. When all gnocchi are cooked, place in oven dish, pour melted butter over them, sprinkle with chopped sage, and add Fontina cheese. Bake in oven preheated to 350°F until cheese has melted completely.

Serve immediately.

Involtini di Melanzane e Fontina
(Rolled Eggplants with Fontina Cheese and Pancetta)

Cesare Franchino, Arvier, Aosta

(Yield: 4 servings)

1 eggplant (cut thin lengthwise, 8 pieces)
4 tablespoons extra-virgin olive oil
8 thin slices pancetta
8 thin slices Fontina cheese
salt and freshly ground pepper (to taste)
½ cup finely chopped Italian parsley

1. Soak eggplant slices in salted water for approx. 30 minutes to remove bitterness, then rinse and pat dry.

2. Warm 2 tablespoons of oil in skillet over medium heat and fry eggplant slices on both sides for approx. 3 minutes each (until tender but still slightly firm). Set aside until all have been cooked.

3. Lay eggplant slice on piece of pancetta, add slice of Fontina, and sprinkle with salt, pepper and parsley (to taste). Roll and secure with toothpick.

4. Warm remaining oil in same skillet over medium heat and cook rolls until cheese is melted, turning often to brown all sides.

Serve immediately. Garnish with more parsley.

You can add some cherry tomatoes as a final garnish.

Filetto Carbonade
(Beef Fillet in Wine Sauce)

Claudia Pellisier, Arvier, Aosta

(Yield: 4 servings)

4 beef fillets (¼ pound each)
1 onion (diced)
1 carrot (diced)
1 celery stalk (diced)
1½ cups red wine (full-bodied)

½ cup butter
3 garlic cloves (minced)
1 rosemary sprig (minced)
salt and freshly ground pepper
polenta for 4 (refer to page 308)

1. In skillet over medium heat, add onions, carrots, celery, wine, and a pinch of salt and pepper. Bring to boil. Cook until softened, transfer to blender and purée. Reserve and keep warm.

2. Melt butter in the same skillet over medium heat. Add garlic and cook until fragrant.

3. Add fillets and sauté with garlic. Add rosemary, salt and pepper (to taste).

4. Serve fillets on top of polenta discs. Garnish with vegetable purée.

Serve immediately.

Polenta Concia alla Valdostana
(Polenta with Layered Cheeses)

Angelo Franchino, Leverogne, Aosta

(Yield: 4 servings)

8½ cups water

3 cups corn flour

½ cup butter (keep cold and diced)

6 ounces Fontina cheese, thinly sliced
(Val D'Aosta if available)

6 ounces Toma cheese, thinly sliced
(Val D'Aosta if available)

salt and freshly ground pepper

1. Make polenta as instructed on page 308.

2. Once polenta is ready, spread it evenly into lightly greased 6x12 baking dish. Allow to cool and solidify for approx. 2 hours.

3. Lightly grease a 6x6 baking dish, halve the polenta, and insert one piece. Add half the cheeses and butter, and a pinch of salt and pepper. Add 2nd layer of polenta. Top off with remaining cheeses.

4. Bake in oven preheated to 350°F for 25 to 30 minutes.

When spreading out the polenta after it has been cooked, any large pan can be used. When assembling the Polenta Concia make sure baking dish has high sides to accept the layers. Our dish was two layers and 2½ xes high; thinner layers can be used in greater numbers.

Involtini di Vitello di Fenis
(Stuffed Veal Rolls)

Ilde Franchino, Arvier, Aosta

Mocetta was originally a cured mountain goat meat, made like prosciutto, which primarily comes from the Valle D'Aosta. Nowadays, it is made mainly with beef, or sometimes farm goats.

(Yield: 4 servings)

4 veal cutlets (make sure the meat is tender)
3 ounces mocetta (4 thin slices)
3 ounces Fontina cheese (4 thin slices)
flour (for dredging)
1 egg (beaten)

½ cup butter
1½ ounces brandy
½ cup cream
salt and freshly ground pepper

1. Place slice of mocetta and slice of Fontina on each veal cutlet.

2. Roll tightly. Secure with toothpick.

3. Dredge each roll in flour and then in egg.

4. Melt butter in skillet over low heat; carefully add brandy and cream, then veal rolls.

5. Cook for approx. 10 minutes, turning rolls a few times and seasoning with salt and pepper.

   Note: when adding any alcohol to a pan on the stove, remove the pan from the heat first, add the alcohol and return the pan to the heat.

Funghi Ripieni
(Stuffed Mushrooms)

Maria Gallo, Arvier, Aosta

(Yield: 4 servings)

12 small porcini mushrooms
4 tablespoons extra-virgin olive oil
4 ounces pancetta (one slice, diced)
2 garlic cloves (minced)
1 tablespoon finely chopped parsley

½ pound boiled potatoes
1 egg
2 ounces Fontina cheese
butter
salt and freshly ground pepper

1. Clean mushrooms and remove stems. Rinse stems thoroughly, dry, and chop finely.

2. Warm oil in skillet over medium heat and sauté pancetta and garlic for a few minutes. Increase heat to high, add chopped mushroom stems and cook for 10 minutes. Remove from heat. Season with salt, pepper and parsley. Set aside.

3. Mix potatoes, egg and cheese in bowl until well-combined. Add reserved mushroom mixture and re-mix.

4. Stuff mixture into mushroom caps, making sure to fill them completely.

5. Place caps in lightly greased baking dish and top each mushroom with dab of butter.

6. Bake in oven preheated to 350°F for approx. 30 minutes.

Serve hot or at room temperature.

We used baby portabella mushrooms in place of the porcini and they are excellent.

Civet di Camoscio
(Wild Goat in Wine)

Tiziana Franchino, Leverogne, Aosta

(Yield: 4 servings)

2 pounds wild goat meat (camois)
(cut in bite size pieces)
MARINADE:
3 cups red wine
1 onion (diced)
1 carrot (diced)
3 garlic cloves (minced)
1 celery stalk (diced)
1 sprig fresh thyme (1 tsp dried)
4 sage leaves

3 bay leaves
3 cloves
1 sprig marjoram (1 tsp dried)
1 teaspoon each salt and freshly ground pepper

Flour (for dredging)
4 tablespoons olive oil
1 tablespoon butter
1 onion (diced)
1 carrot (diced)

1. Rinse meat under cold water and pat thoroughly dry.

2. Place meat and marinade ingredients in large bowl.

3. Cover with plastic wrap and marinade for approx. 12 hours in fridge. Stir occasionally.

4. Drain. Reserve liquid.

5. Dredge meat in flour, shaking off excess.

6. Warm oil and butter in large skillet over medium heat. Add diced onions and carrots, and cook until onions are translucent.

7. Add meat and braise on all sides. Cover meat with reserved liquid and cook with lid on for approx. 2 hours over low heat.

8. Add additional reserved marinade (or water) as required, making sure the meat does not dry out.

Serve with polenta (as instructed on page 308).

EMILIA-ROMAGNA

CAPITAL

Bologna

RED WINE

Lambrusco

WHITE WINE

Trebbiano

Valle D'Aosta

Piemonte

Liguria

Lombardia

Trentino-Alto Adige

Friuli-Venezia Giulia

Veneto

Emilia-Romagna

Ligurian Sea

Toscana

Marche

Umbria

Adriatic Sea

Lazio

Abruzzo

Molise

Sardegna

Campania

Puglia

Basilicata

Mediterranean Sea

Tyrrhenian Sea

Calabria

Sicilia

Ionian Sea

Penne alla Boscaiola
(Penne with Sausage and Porcini Mushrooms)

Eva (Sorrentino) Gigi, Bologna

(Yield: 4 servings)

1 pound penne rigate
2 tablespoons extra-virgin olive oil
6 cups Porcini mushrooms (thinly sliced)
1 onion (thinly sliced)
½ pound mild Italian sausage (casing removed)

salt and freshly ground pepper
½ cup dry white wine
12 ounces puréed tomatoes
1½ cups cream (half and half)
Pecorino Romano or Parmigiano-Reggiano

1. Warm oil in large skillet over medium heat. Add mushrooms and onions. Cook until onions are slightly golden but not brown (5 to 7 minutes).

2. Add sausage (crumbled), salt and pepper, and wine. Cook until wine has evaporated.

3. Add tomatoes and continue cooking for approx. 10 minutes. Add cream and mix thoroughly. Cook for another 5 minutes.

4. Meanwhile, in pot of salted boiling water, cook pasta until al dente.

5. Drain pasta, reserving approx. 1 cup of liquid. Add pasta to skillet. Increase heat to medium-high.

6. Mix thoroughly, adding some of reserved liquid if too thick.

   Remove the skillet from the heat and add a good handful of cheese, mix again, and serve immediately.

Triglia alla Livornese
(Mullet in Tomato Sauce)

Filomena (Busi) Pazini, Vasti, Parma

(Yield: 4 servings)

8 mullet fillets (bones removed)
flour (for dredging)
5 tablespoons extra-virgin olive oil (divided)
2 garlic cloves (minced)

1 tablespoon chopped fresh italian parsley
1 pound tomatoes (skin removed, diced)
salt and freshly ground pepper

1. Season fillets and dredge in flour, shaking off excess. Set aside.

2. Warm 2 tablespoons of oil in skillet over medium heat. Add garlic and parsley. Cook until fragrant (approx. 30 seconds).

3. Add tomatoes. Simmer for approx. 20 minutes.

4. While sauce is cooking, heat remainder of oil in skillet over medium heat and fry mullet fillets for approx. 3 minutes per side.

5. Plate fillets, top with tomato sauce, season with salt and pepper to taste, and garnish with fresh parsley.

Serve immediately.

Cappelletti in Brodo
(Cappelletti in Broth)

Elisa Maranini, Ferrara

Cappelletti is the plural of *cappelletto*, which literally means "little hat," – which is what this type of pasta resembles.

(Yield: 4 servings)

FILLING:

6 tablespoons butter

3 ounces ground pork

6 ounces ground beef

6 ounces ground veal

2 eggs

1 cup breadcrumbs

6 ounces prosciutto (diced fine)

1 cup grated Parmesan cheese

1 teaspoon freshly grated nutmeg

salt

egg dough (see page 306)

9 cups broth (chicken or beef)

1. Have meats ground fine by your butcher.

2. Melt butter in skillet over medium heat. Add pork, beef, and veal. Cook for approx. 10 minutes. Set aside and allow to reach room temperature.

3. When completely cooled, add eggs and breadcrumbs and combine well. Add prosciutto, Parmesan cheese and nutmeg. Salt to taste and mix again. If too dry, add a little broth.

4. Prepare the egg dough.

5. Roll out thin sheets of dough and cut into 2-inch squares.

6. In centre of each square, place a little stuffing and fold into triangle, pressing down on seams to seal. Holding the two sides, form cappelletti.

7. Bring broth to boil in large saucepan. Add cappelletti and cook for approx. 3 minutes. When they rise to the surface they are cooked.

Serve while warm, topped with grated Parmesan cheese.

Tartine alla Robiola
(Robiola Spread)

Gioachino Busi, Vasti, Parma

There are two cheeses that go by the name of Robiola. There is one from Piedmont, which is a fresh cheese, and one from Lombardia, which is of a tan colour. The latter is rich and mildly pungent.

½ pound Robiola (fresh cheese)
2 tablespoons butter (room temperature)
4 ounces dry white wine
Saltines or toasted bread

1. Combine cheese and butter in bowl and mix thoroughly.

2. Add wine and continue mixing until creamy and paste-like.

3. Transfer to serving bowl, and serve with toasted bread, saltines, or your favourite cracker.

Robiola cheese may be difficult to find. The best substitute would be ½ cup of Mascarpone with 1/3 cup of Ricotta.

Gnocchi di Zucca al Semolino
(Semolina Pumpkin Gnocchi)

Elisa Marinini, Ferrara

(Yield: 4 servings)

2 pounds pumpkin
(peeled and cubed into 1-inch pieces)
1 onion (diced)
5 tablespoons butter
salt
2 cups semolina flour

1 egg yolk
1 tablespoon butter
SAGE SAUCE:
12 sage leaves (chopped)
2 tablespoons butter
grated Parmesan cheese

1. Melt butter in saucepan over medium heat. Add pumpkin cubes and onions. Cook for approx. 30 minutes. Salt (to taste) and add a little water if too dry.

2. Purée mixture in food processor. Once completely cooled, add egg and pulse a few times. Add flour and pulse until dough-like and pulling away from sides.

3. Place onto floured surface and, working with small batches at a time, roll into ½-inch cylinders and cut into inch-long pieces. Using the end of a fork, you can give it the gnocchi look.

4. Place the gnocchi on a lightly floured cookie sheet until ready to use.

5. Bring large pot of salted water to boil. Add gnocchi, making sure not to crowd. When they rise to the surface they are cooked.

6. Remove first batch with slotted spoon and continue.

Serve warm with sage sauce and grated Parmesan cheese.

Sage Sauce: Melt butter in skillet over medium heat, add sage leaves and cook until slightly crisp. Pour over gnocchi.

Asparagi alla Panna
(Creamy Asparagus)

Gioachino Busi, Vasti, Parma

(Yield: 4 servings)

2 pounds asparagus (cleaned and trimmed)
flour as needed
4 eggs (beaten)

breadcrumbs as needed
2 tablespoons extra-virgin olive oil
salt and freshly ground pepper

1. Prepare bowl of ice water and set aside.

2. Bring saucepan of salted water to boil, add asparagus and cook for approx. 3 minutes.

3. Drain asparagus and immediately immerse into bowl of ice water to stop cooking process.

4. Once asparagus is cooled, cut in half lengthwise.

5. In 3 separate bowls prepare flour, eggs and breadcrumbs.

6. Begin by dredging asparagus in flour, then dip into egg and finally roll in breadcrumbs.

7. Warm oil in large skillet over medium heat. Add asparagus and cook until lightly golden.

Remove, season with salt and pepper and serve immediately.

Fettine al Pomodoro
(Veal Cutlets in Tomato Sauce)

Filomena (Busi) Pazini, Vasti, Parma

(Yield: 4 servings)

4 boneless veal top round steaks or cutlets
(6 ounces each)
SAUCE:
4 tablespoons extra-virgin olive oil
2 tomatoes (seeds removed, diced)

2 garlic cloves (minced)
2 fresh oregano sprigs
salt and freshly ground pepper

1. Flatten veal with kitchen mallet to ¼-inch thickness. Season with salt and pepper. Set aside.

2. Warm oil in skillet over medium heat and cook cutlets (fettine) for approx. 2 minutes per side. Set aside.

3. In same skillet add tomatoes, garlic, and oregano. Once boiling, reduce heat to low and simmer for approx. 15 minutes.

4. Season with salt and pepper.

5. Add fettine to sauce and cook for another 5 minutes.

Serve along with rice (as instructed on page 306) or mixed vegetables.

Baccalà Bolognese
(Salted Cod Bolognese Style)

Eva (Sorrentino) Gigi, Bologna

(Yield: 4 servings)

2 pounds cod (cut into 2-inch pieces)
2 tablespoons extra-virgin olive oil (+ extra)
1 onion (diced)
2 garlic cloves (minced)
4 tomatoes (diced)
1 bay leaf
½ cup water

½ cup white wine
4 potatoes (cut into ½-inch cubes)
19 ounces cannellini beans (canned)
19 ounces chickpeas (canned)
salt and freshly ground pepper
2 tablespoons roughly chopped parsley

1. Warm oil in large skillet over medium heat. Cook onions and garlic until onions are translucent. Add tomatoes.

2. Once boiling, add bay leaf, water, wine, potatoes, beans, and chickpeas. Cook until potatoes are fork-tender but still firm.

3. Add cod and oil. Cook partially covered for approx. 15 minutes.

Season with salt and pepper to taste. Serve garnished with parsley.

Tagliatelle al Sugo di Piselli
(Tagliatelle with Peas in Sauce)

Elisa Maranini, Ferrara

(Yield: 4 servings)

1 pound tagliatelle (packaged or
homemade: see pasta recipe on pages 306-7)
4 tablespoons extra-virgin olive oil
1 onion (diced)
1 celery stalk (diced)

1½ cups fresh peas
3 cups crushed or puréed tomato
salt and freshly ground pepper
Parmigiano cheese

1. Warm oil in large skillet over medium heat. Add onions and celery. Cook until onions are translucent. Add peas and continue cooking for another 5 minutes. Season with salt and pepper. Then add tomatoes, stirring often.

2. Once boiling, reduce heat to low and allow to simmer for approx. 20 minutes (add a little water if it thickens too much).

3. While sauce is cooking, bring large pot of salted water to boil.

4. Add tagliatelle and cook until al dente. Drain. Add pasta to skillet. Mix well.

Serve with freshly grated Parmigiano cheese.

Involtini di Lucchesia
(Zucchini Rolls in Tomato Sauce)

Maria (Busi) Opimitti, Vasti, Parma

(Yield: 4 servings)

4 zucchini (sliced lengthwise ¼-inch thick)
3½ tablespoons butter
1 pound ground beef
1 egg

3 tablespoons grated Parmigiano
salt and freshly ground pepper
2 tablespoons extra-virgin olive oil
1½ cups peeled and diced tomatoes

1. Melt butter in skillet over medium heat. Fry zucchini for approx. 3 minutes on each side. Remove and set aside on paper towels. Allow to cool.

2. Combine beef, egg, cheese, salt and pepper in bowl. Mix thoroughly and form into small meatballs (as many as the zucchini slices).

3. When zucchini slices have cooled, wrap around meatballs. Secure with a toothpick. Place in greased oven dish and bake in oven preheated to 300°F for 15 minutes.

4. While zucchini rolls are baking, add oil to zucchini skillet and cook tomatoes over medium heat. Season with salt and pepper and simmer until zucchini rolls are cooked.

5. Plate and pour the tomato sauce overtop.

Re-season with salt and pepper to taste and serve immediately.

LIGURIA

CAPITAL

Genova

RED WINE

Rossese

WHITE WINE

Cinque Terre (Tigullio Bianco)

Farinata Genovese
(Chickpea Biscuits)

Carlo Luigi Mazza, Genova

(Yield: 4 servings)

1 pound chickpea flour

4 cups water

1 teaspoon salt

1 teaspoon finely chopped rosemary

½ cup extra-virgin olive oil

extra-virgin olive oil for drizzling

1. In large bowl and using electric mixer, add ingredients to flour one at a time, ensuring each is fully incorporated before adding the next. Mixture should be smooth after approx. 10 minutes.

2. Grease medium-size cookie sheet with butter and pour mixture evenly onto it, to height of no more than ¾ of an inch.

3. Bake in oven preheated to 350°F until top starts to turn lightly brown. Remove from oven.

4. Cut into squares, rectangles or any shape you like.

Serve warm, drizzled with extra-virgin olive oil, or at room temperature with soup.

Zuppa di Cozze
(Mussel Soup)

Giancarlo Roffi, La Spezia

(Yield: 6 servings)

4 pounds mussels (scrubbed and washed)
2 tablespoons extra-virgin olive oil
2 garlic cloves (minced)
3 tablespoons finely chopped parsley
½ lemon (juiced)

½ cup dry white wine
1 cup water
salt and freshly ground pepper
6 slices day-old Italian bread (1½-inches thick)

1. Place mussels in saucepan over medium heat. Cover and allow to steam in their own juices for approx. 10 minutes.

2. Strain mussel liquid and reserve.

3. Warm oil in skillet over low heat. Add garlic. Cook until fragrant (approx. 30 seconds). Stir in parsley, lemon juice, reserved mussel liquid, wine and water. Cook for another 5 minutes.

4. Season with salt and pepper to taste.

5. Place slice of toasted bread in each bowl and pour in some liquid. Top with mussels.

Serve immediately.

When cooking mussels, discard any that have not opened.

Polenta con Cavoli e Fagioli
(Polenta with Cabbage and Beans)

Carlo Luigi Mazza, Genova

(Yield: 4 servings)

6 cups water
2 cups Romano beans (preferably fresh)
¼ head cabbage (finely sliced)
other fresh vegetables as desired

1 teaspoon salt
1½ cups cornmeal
1 tablespoon extra-virgin olive oil

1. Bring 6 cups of water in saucepan to boil. Add beans, cabbage and salt. Cook until beans are slightly soft (approx. 10 minutes).

2. Reduce heat to low and slowly add cornmeal. Stir continuously until mixture thickens (20 to 30 minutes).

3. Remove from heat, add oil and stir for another minute.

4. Pour mixture in medium-size rectangular baking dish. Allow mixture to set until firm (approx. an hour or overnight).

When cooking the cornmeal (polenta) add additional hot water if necessary.

Acciughe al Limone
(Lemon-marinated Anchovies)

Cristina Roffi, La Spezia

(Yield: 6 servings)

1 pound fresh anchovies
6 lemons (juiced)
salt and freshly ground pepper
¼ cup extra-virgin olive oil
1 tablespoon finely chopped parsley
zest of 1 lemon

1. Remove heads from anchovies, open, clean, and debone.

2. Wash and pat dry. Place in a deep dish.

3. Pour in lemon juice, season with salt and pepper, and refrigerate wrapped for approx. 2 hours.

4. Just prior to serving, drain off juices, pour oil over fillets, and sprinkle with parsley and lemon zest.

Polpettone di Zucchini
(Zucchini Loaf)

Carlo Luigi Mazza, Genova

(Yield: 6 servings)

½ cup milk
2 cups breadcrumbs (extra for pan)
½ cup extra-virgin olive oil
10 medium zucchini
(cut into 1/8-inch rounds)

4 eggs
¾ cup grated Romano cheese
2 garlic cloves (minced)
¼ cup each basil and parsley (chopped fine)
1 teaspoon each salt and freshly ground pepper

1. Warm milk in small saucepan (do not boil). Add breadcrumbs, remove from heat. Mix well, and set aside.

2. Warm oil in skillet over medium heat, fry zucchini rounds for approx. 1 minute per side, making sure not to overcook. Set aside to cool completely.

3. In large bowl, beat eggs until fluffed. Add cooled zucchini, breadcrumb mixture, cheese, garlic, basil, parsley, salt and pepper. Mix until combined. Set aside.

4. Grease loaf pan. Add enough breadcrumbs to line bottom and sides. Pour in zucchini mixture, packing evenly, and top with more breadcrumbs.

5. Bake in oven preheated to 350°F for approx. 1½ hours or until an inserted toothpick comes out clean.

6. Remove from oven and let sit for approx. 30 minutes before slicing.

Serve as a replacement for bread with soup.

Trenette al Pesto
(Trenette with Pesto, Potatoes and Green Beans)

Giancarlo Roffi, La Spezia

Trenette noodles are narrow, flat, and commonly confused with fettuccine or tagliatelle; however, trenette noodles are not made with eggs, and have one side that is curled.

(Yield: 6 servings)

1 pound trenette
PESTO:
1 cup fresh basil leaves (tightly packed)
2 tablespoons pine nuts
3 garlic cloves (peeled)
salt

3 tablespoons grated Pecorino
or Parmesan cheese
½ cup extra-virgin olive oil

2 medium potatoes
1 pound green beans (trimmed)

1. Wash basil leaves and dry well.

2. In food processor, add basil, pine nuts, garlic, a pinch of salt, the cheeses and a small amount of oil. Purée. Pour in remaining oil, blend for few more seconds, and reserve.

3. Peel potatoes and cut into julienne strips. Set aside.

4. Bring large pot of salted water to boil. Add green beans and cook for 5 minutes.

5. Add potatoes. After 2 minutes add noodles.

6. When noodles are cooked al dente, drain and place in large serving bowl. Add prepared pesto. Mix well.

Serve immediately with freshly grated Pecorino or Parmesan cheese. In this recipe penne was used.

Riso con Zucchini al Forno
(Rice and Zucchini Casserole)

Carlo Luigi Mazza, Genova

(Yield: 4 servings)

2 cups arborio rice
½ cup extra-virgin olive oil
1 onion (diced)
3 garlic cloves (minced)

3 medium zucchini (diced)
1 cup grated Romano cheese
½ cup cream or whole milk
salt and freshly ground pepper

1. Bring pot of salted water to boil and cook rice until al dente (as instructed on page 306). Drain and set aside in large bowl.

2. Warm oil in skillet over medium heat. Add onions and garlic. Cook until onions are translucent. Add zucchini and continue cooking for another 5 minutes.

3. To the bowl with rice, add cooked zucchini mixture, cheese, cream, salt and pepper (to taste). Mix well.

4. Add mixture to a lightly greased baking dish and bake in oven preheated to 350°F for approx. 45 minutes, or until top turns golden.

Serve immediately, topped with freshly grated Romano cheese.

Torta di Bietole
(Swiss Chard Quiche)

Carlo Luigi Mazza, Genova

(Yield: 4 servings)

pie dough (see page 308)
FILLING:
2 pounds Swiss chard
2 eggs (beaten)

½ cup grated Parmesan or Romano cheese
favourite herbs (thyme, marjoram, nutmeg)
salt and freshly ground pepper

1. Prepare pie dough. Divide in two, 2/3 for bottom and 1/3 for top.

2. Wash chard thoroughly. Cut out centre stems and chop leaves into strips approx. 1 inch wide and 1½ to 2 inches long.

3. In pot of salted boiling water, first add chopped stems. Cook for approx. 3 minutes, then add leaves and continue cooking until wilted but not fully cooked (approx. another 3 minutes).

4. Strain until most of liquid is drained and reserve chard.

5. Grease 9-inch pie dish (bottom and sides) and cover with rolled-out pie dough, allowing an extra ½ inch all around.

6. Add eggs, cheese, herbs, salt and pepper in a bowl. Mix thoroughly. Add Swiss chard to egg mixture and combine well.

7. Place mixture in dish, packing evenly all around. Add remaining dough to top and crimple edges to seal. Make a few slits on top with a knife.

8. Bake in a preheated oven, on centre rack, at 350°F until top is golden (approx. 30 minutes).

You can substitute baby artichokes or any favourite greens for Swiss chard.

Minestrone Genovese
(Minestrone)

Carlo Luigi Mazza, Genova

This was how my mother made this, and as with all Italian dishes, it was basically done by eye and taste. —Carlo

(Yield: 4 servings)

6 tablespoons extra-virgin olive oil
2 cups Romano beans
3 potatoes (¾-inch cubes)
3 carrots (diced)
1 onion (diced)
1 tomato (skin removed, ¾-inch cubes)
1 cup green beans (¾-inch lengths)

1 tablespoon salt
1 teaspoon freshly ground pepper
2 beef bones (fist size) – optional
3 tablespoons pesto
(Genovese or your favourite, page 307)
1 pound short tube noodles

1. Warm oil in large saucepan over medium heat. Add beans, potatoes, carrots, onion, tomatoes, green beans, salt and pepper. Cook for approx. 3 minutes.

2. Add beef bones and enough water to cover all by one inch.

3. Once boiling, add pesto and stir well. Reduce heat to simmer and cook partially covered for approx. 1 hour, or until vegetables are tender.

4. Discard bones and add pasta. Increase heat to medium and continue cooking until pasta is al dente.

Serve immediately.

If you are using dry beans, allow them to soak overnight. To make peeling the tomato easier drop into boiling water for approx. 1 minute. As an alternative to beef bones, replace water and bones with chicken stock.

Foglie di Lattuga Ripiene in Brodo
(Stuffed Lettuce Leaves in Broth)

Cristina Roffi, La Spezia

(Yield: 4 servings)

1 Romaine lettuce head
STUFFING:
1 ounce dried porcini mushrooms
2 tablespoon fresh marjoram leaves
2 garlic cloves
1 cup coarse breadcrumbs, soaked in milk and squeezed dry
2 eggs

¼ cup freshly grated Parmesan cheese
salt and freshly ground pepper

1 egg white (beaten)
6 tablespoons extra-virgin olive oil
5 cups broth (chicken or beef)
4 slices day-old Italian bread

1. Remove outside leaves of lettuce and extract heart. Wash and dry 12 leaves and set aside.

2. Soak mushrooms in lukewarm water for 30 minutes.

3. Drain mushrooms and chop along with lettuce heart. Combine with stuffing ingredients. Mix. Set aside.

4. Bring pot of water to boil, drop in 12 lettuce leaves, and blanch for approx. 1 minute. Carefully remove leaves and place on clean towel. Pat dry.

5. Starting at large end of leaf, add some prepared stuffing. Brush inside leaf with egg white.

6. Fold in sides and lightly roll (they should look like a small package). Insert a toothpick to secure.

7. Warm 2 tablespoons of oil and 1 cup of broth in skillet over low heat. Add lettuce rolls and cook covered for a few minutes, turning occasionally. Bring rest of broth to boil in separate saucepan.

8. Brush slices of bread with remaining oil and toast in oven preheated to 350°F until golden.

9. Place slice of bread in bottom of each soup bowl, top with 3 lettuce rolls, and fill with hot broth.

Season with salt and freshly ground pepper. Serve immediately.

Spigola al Sale
(Sea Bass Baked in Salt)

Giancarlo Roffi, La Spezia

The simplicity of this dish is unbelievable, with a foolproof finish.

(Yield: 6 servings)

4 pounds sea bass, salmon or grouper
3 rosemary sprigs
salt and freshly ground pepper
4 pounds coarse sea salt
1 cup flour

½ cup water
¼ cup extra-virgin olive oil
SAUCE:
2 tablespoon butter
juice from 1 lemon
1 tablespoon chopped parsley

1. Clean out cavity of fish (leaving skin on). Insert sprig of rosemary, add salt and pepper, and re-close.

2. In large bowl with sea salt, add water and mix until snow-like.

3. Line baking sheet with parchment paper and layer with approx. ¼-inch of salt mixture. Place fish on top. Add rosemary sprigs, one each above and below.

4. Cover fish completely with remaining sea salt. Shape to contour of fish and pack firmly.

5. Mix flour and water into thin paste and brush it over packed salt.

6. Bake in preheated oven, on middle rack, at 400°F for approx. 30 minutes.

7. Remove sheet from oven. Allow to rest while making sauce.

8. Warm oil and butter in skillet over low heat. Add lemon juice and parsley. Season with salt and pepper. Cook for a few minutes then transfer to dipping bowl.

9. Crack crust and transfer fish to a serving platter, peeling back skin.

Serve immediately.

Although we only used rosemary, an assortment of herbs and spices can be added to the cavity of the fish.

TOSCANA

CAPITAL
Firenze

RED WINE
Chianti or Brunello di Montalcino

WHITE WINE
Vernaccia di San Gemignano

Minestrone di Farro della Garfagnana
(Minestrone with Spelt)

Maria Rosa (Lunardi) Conti, Pontecosi, Lucca

This is a very rustic hearty Tuscan dish. It was taught to me by my cousin Maria Rosa (Lunardi) Conti, in a small hamlet town of Pontecosi in the remote northern Garfagnana region of Tuscany. In her recipe she used everything fresh, including beans and vegetables straight from the garden, and potatoes from the rich soil of their vineyard. Even the chicken stock was made from scratch the night before. The recipe here shows my shortcuts. —Giuliano

(Yield: 10 servings)

4 ounces pancetta (diced)
2 tablespoons (plus extra) extra-virgin olive oil
8 garlic cloves (minced)
2 onions (diced)
4 carrots (diced)
4 celery stalks (diced)
3 potatoes (diced)

3 cans of beans, 15 ounces each, rinsed (romano, kidney and cannellini)
1 28-ounce can peeled tomatoes
10 cups chicken stock
1 cup spelt (soaked for several hours)
salt and freshly ground pepper
Romano or Parmigiano grated cheese

1. Cook pancetta over medium heat in large saucepan. Add 2 tablespoons of olive oil, garlic and onion. Cook until onions are translucent.

2. Add carrots, celery, potatoes, beans, tomatoes, and chicken stock. Once boiling, reduce heat to simmer and cover for 20 minutes.

3. Once cooked, run everything through *passatutto* (vegetable mill).

4. Return to saucepan, add spelt, stir and cook over low heat for another 20 to 30 minutes. Season with salt and pepper (to taste).

5. When serving, drizzle with extra-virgin olive oil. Sprinkle with cheese and serve with a slice of crusty bread and homemade wine.

To get the right consistency, do not use a blender in place of the passatutto (vegetable mill). To make a heartier version, chop vegetables into ¾-inch cubes, but do not pass through passatutto.

Broccoli Romani
(Roman Broccoli)

Piera Bertoncini, Barga, Lucca

(Yield: 4 servings)

1 head broccoli
2 tablespoons extra-virgin olive oil
2 garlic cloves (slivered)
salt and freshly ground pepper
½ cup white wine

1. Clean broccoli head. Cut off florets, leaving 1½-inch stems.

2. Warm oil in large skillet over medium heat, add garlic slivers, and cook until fragrant (approx. 30 seconds).

3. Add broccoli florets. Increase heat to medium-high. Season with salt and pepper. Mix well and cook covered for approx. 10 minutes.

4. After 6 minutes, add wine and continue cooking until the alcohol has evaporated.

Serve immediately.

Pappardelle con Ragù
(Wide Fettuccine with Meat Sauce)

Leonardo and Lori Andreucci, Castelnuovo di Garfagnana, Lucca

While travelling through Tuscany, we stayed with friends (the Andreucci family) who own the B&B "Da Carlino." They take pride in their local, fresh menu that changes daily. Here is one of their popular recipes which they were happy to share with us. —Giuliano and Caterina.

(Yield: 4 servings)

SAUCE:
2 tablespoons extra-virgin olive oil
1 onion (diced)
1 pound ground pork
½ cup white wine
7 cups tomato sauce (56 ounces) (see page 308)
1½ cups dried porcini mushrooms
(soaked in warm water)

1 rosemary sprig (chopped fine)
salt and freshly ground pepper

1 pound pappardelle
½ cup grated Romano cheese

1. Warm oil in large skillet over medium heat and sauté onions until translucent.

2. Add pork, cooking until brown. Add wine and stir until alcohol is evaporated.

3. Add tomato sauce and mushrooms. Once boiling, reduce heat to low simmer.

4. Add rosemary. Season with salt and pepper. Cook partially covered for 1 hour.

5. When sauce is ready, in pot of salted boiling water add pappardelle and cook until al dente.

6. Drain and add pappardelle to skillet. Remove from heat and add a good handful of cheese. Mix well.

Serve topped with more cheese.

Best made with fresh homemade egg noodles, (pages 306-7).

Ossobuco

Liliana (Salotti) Lunardi, Piano di Coreglia, Lucca

During the Christmas season, our family prepares this recipe in place of the standard turkey and everyone looks forward to it. This was once considered a peasant dish of northern Italy.

(Yield: 4 servings)

1 tablespoon extra-virgin olive oil	1 cup tomato sauce (see page 308)
4 garlic cloves (chopped)	1 cup dry white wine
4 1½-inch cross-cut veal shanks	salt and freshly ground pepper
1 cup flour (for dredging)	

Meat:

1. Warm oil in large Dutch oven over medium heat. Add garlic, and cook until fragrant (approx. 30 seconds).

2. Dredge veal shanks in flour and braise in Dutch oven, 2 to 3 minutes per side.

3. Add ¾ cup each tomato sauce and wine. Ensure veal is submerged.

4. Lower heat to simmer and cook covered for 30 to 40 minutes. Keep meat submerged. Add remaining wine and sauce if necessary. Season with salt and pepper to taste.

Vegetables:

½ cup extra-virgin olive oil	2½ cups diced tomatoes (15 ounces)
½ cup onions (diced)	2 bay leaves
½ cup carrots (diced)	1 teaspoon each finely chopped, rosemary, sage and thyme
½ cup celery (diced)	
4 garlic cloves (minced)	2½ cups precooked Romano beans (15 ounce can drained and rinsed)
½ cup white wine	
4 cups beef broth	salt and pepper

1. Warm oil in large saucepan over medium heat and sauté onions, carrots, celery and garlic.

2. Add wine, bring to simmer. Reduce by half.

3. Add broth, tomatoes and herbs. Simmer until reduced by half.

4. Add beans. Cook for approx. 20 minutes. Season with salt and pepper to taste.

5. When serving, use slotted spoon and bed vegetable mixture on plate. Place ossobuco on top. Ladle sauce over all to taste.

You may cook the ossobuco with the vegetables, but I find it tastes better cooked separately.

Crostini di Fegatini
(Liver Pate)

Leonardo and Lori Andreucci, Castelnuovo di Garfagnana, Lucca

(Yield: 10 to 12 servings)

2 tablespoons extra-virgin olive oil
¼ cup onion (sliced thin)
1 pound chicken liver (cleaned and rinsed)
½ cup capers (in liquid)

4 fresh anchovies
1 tablespoon tomato sauce
white wine
salt and freshly ground pepper

1. Warm oil in medium-size skillet over low heat and sauté onions and liver, stirring continuously for approx. 10 minutes.

2. Remove onions and liver pieces and chop roughly.

3. Using a food processor pulse mixture along with capers (reserving caper juice) until sauce is smooth. Occasionally scrape down sides.

4. Return mixture to skillet over low heat. Add anchovies and cook until anchovies break up and everything is well-incorporated.

5. Add tomato sauce and 1 tablespoon of liquid from capers. Stir often. Cook for approx. 15 minutes. Add wine to keep moist if necessary.

6. Once consistency is spread-like, remove from heat and allow to cool. Season with salt and pepper to taste.

Spread on crusty, toasted Italian bread.
Great appetizer.

Insalata di Farro
(Spelt Salad)

Silvana Bertoncini, Barga, Lucca

(Yield: 4 servings)

1 cup spelt
12 cherry tomatoes (halved)
2 green onions (diced, green and white parts)
2 tablespoons parsley finely chopped
8 basil leaves (chiffonaded)
extra-virgin olive oil
salt and freshly ground pepper

1. In pot of salted boiling water, add spelt and cook 15 to 20 minutes.

2. Drain. Rinse under cold water and allow to sit in colander until most water is gone.

3. Add tomatoes, green onions, parsley and basil in bowl. Season with salt and pepper. Mix thoroughly.

4. Add drained spelt and drizzle with olive oil. Toss everything gently. Re-season with salt and pepper if necessary.

5. Cover bowl with plastic wrap and allow to cool in fridge before serving.

This is a very refreshing meal that is normally served in the summer months.

Baccalà Marinato
(Marinated Salted Cod)

Remo and Fiorella Dolfi, Marina di Carrara, Massa-Carrara

(Yield: 8 servings)

2 pounds baccalà (dried codfish)

flour for dredging

1½ cups extra-virgin olive oil

2 garlic cloves (minced)

2 rosemary sprigs (minced)

2 teaspoons tomato paste

1½ cups white vinegar

1½ cup white wine

1. Prepare baccalà as per instructions on page 306.

2. Once prepared, cut cod in 3-inch fillets and pat dry.

3. Dredge each piece in flour, shaking off excess.

4. Warm oil in large skillet over medium heat and cook cod fillets until slightly golden (3 to 4 minutes per side). Remove from pan and set aside in large bowl.

5. In same skillet over medium heat, add remaining oil, garlic and rosemary. Cook until fragrant (approx. 30 seconds).

6. Add tomato paste. Cook for approx. 3 minutes, stirring often. Add vinegar and wine. Reduce heat to low and cook for approx. 20 minutes.

7. Pour the sauce over cod in a bowl, cover with aluminum foil, and cool to room temperature.

This is best made the day before. Allowing it to sit overnight brings out all the flavours.

Topetti
(Stuffed Zucchini Flowers)

Ghisola (Biagi) Bertini, Bagni di Lucca, Lucca

When I was a child, my mother use to make these when the zucchini flowers were in bloom. —Silvano

(Yield: 4 servings)

24 zucchini flowers
(cleaned and with stems on)
FILLING:
1½ pounds lean ground beef
2 eggs
½ cup grated Parmigiano or Romano cheese
3 garlic cloves (minced)

1 tablespoon finely chopped fresh oregano
1 teaspoon each salt and freshly ground pepper

2 tablespoons extra-virgin olive oil
2½ cups tomatoes (diced or 15 ounce can)
1½ cups tomato sauce

1. In large bowl, thoroughly mix beef, eggs, cheese, garlic, oregano, salt and pepper. Use mixture to stuff zucchini flowers. Leave room to fold ends of flowers closed so filling does not fall out.

2. Oil large oven dish and place stuffed flowers in a single layer. Leave room between each flower.

3. Fill small open spaces with diced tomatoes and then cover with tomato sauce, ensuring flowers are almost fully covered.

4. Place dish on centre rack in oven preheated to 350°F. Bake for approx. 30 minutes or until cooked.

Serve hot with a layer of cheese.

Sometimes my mother would fry the zucchini flowers instead of baking them. Both ways are great. When in season, most markets have zucchini flowers, but with a little patience you can grow them yourself and enjoy not just the flowers but the zucchini as well.

When they are cooked and plated, the stem of the flower looks like the tail of a mouse, hence the name "Topi" or "Topetti" (little mouse).

Risotto di Farro ai Funghi Secchi
(Spelt Risotto with Dried Mushrooms)

Caterina (Iatonna) Lunardi, Windsor, Ontario

This dish is a simple variant of traditional Tuscan spelt dishes. It is served mostly in the northern region of Tuscany. We discovered this dish in a little bistro full of locals in the hills just above Collodi, where the fable of Pinocchio is said to have taken place. This dish can be made with fresh porcini when in season.

—Caterina

(Yield: 4 servings)

1 pound spelt
¾ cup dried porcini mushrooms
2 tablespoons butter
2 garlic cloves (minced)

½ cup milk
salt and freshly ground pepper
Parmesan cheese (grated)

1. Soak porcini mushrooms in 1¼ cups warm water for 30 min.

2. In pot of salted boiling water cook spelt for approx. 20 minutes. Drain and set aside. (Reserve 1 cup of liquid.)

3. Melt butter in skillet over medium heat. Add garlic, mushrooms, and reserved liquid. Sauté for approx. 5 minutes.

4. Add spelt and milk. Season with salt and pepper. Cook for another 5 minutes.

5. Remove from heat and add handful of cheese (to taste). Mix well.

Serve topped with additional cheese.

La Farinata
(Polenta Bean Soup)

Franca (Salotti) Giacomelli, Pescia, Pistoia

We accidentally stumbled across this dish as we were driving from my cousin's home in Pescia to a nightclub in Montecatini, in a small town called Buggiano. We pulled over for a bite to eat and the local special was "la farinata." The next morning I had to have my aunt teach me the recipe. —Giuliano

(Yield: 6 servings)

1 pound Borlotti beans (soaked overnight)

2 garlic cloves (whole and peeled)

1 garlic clove (thinly sliced)

½ cup (plus 1 tablespoon) extra-virgin olive oil

2 onions (thinly sliced)

2 celery stalks (thinly sliced)

4 carrots (thinly sliced)

20 kale leaves (thinly sliced)

½ head white cabbage (thinly sliced)

3 ripe tomatoes (diced)

1 vegetable stock cube

2 cups cornmeal

salt and freshly ground pepper

1. In saucepan over medium heat add soaked beans, 4 cups water, 2 garlic cloves and 1 tablespoon of oil. Once boiling, lower to simmer and cook until beans are soft.

2. Blend half the mixture in a food processor, then pour into unblended beans. Stir and set aside.

3. Warm remaining oil in large saucepan over medium heat. Add onions and sliced garlic. Cook until garlic is fragrant. Add celery, carrots, kale and cabbage. Cook for 10 minutes.

4. Add tomatoes. Once boiling, lower heat to simmer and cook for approx. 30 minutes.

5. Add bean mixture (step #2) and vegetable-stock cube. Stir well and add sufficient water to submerge all by approx. 3 inches. Once boiling, add cornmeal slowly. Stir constantly to avoid lumps. Cook 20 minutes, adding water to thin as needed. Season with salt and freshly ground pepper (to taste).

Serve with a drizzle of extra-virgin olive oil on top.

This is a great fall-season dish. Canned beans can be substituted if necessary.

MARCHE

CAPITAL

Ancona

RED WINE

Rosso Conero

WHITE WINE

Verdicchio

Passatelli
(Passatelli Pasta/Soup)

Emilia (Giuliani) Vagnini, Fano, Pesaro-Urbino

Passatelli is pasta made with eggs, breadcrumbs, Parmesan cheese (though this recipe uses Grana Padano) and nutmeg. Flour is not one of the ingredients.

(Yield: 4 servings)

8 eggs

3½ cups breadcrumbs

1½ cups grated Grana Padano cheese

3½ tablespoons butter (room temperature)

1/8 teaspoon freshly grated nutmeg

1 lemon zest

6 cups chicken broth

1. As if making pasta dough, incorporate eggs, breadcrumbs, cheese, butter, nutmeg and lemon zest into large bowl using an electric mixer. Add one ingredient at a time.

2. Once firm, pass dough through passatelli maker. Cut links into 3-inch lengths.

3. In large saucepan bring chicken broth to boil. Add passatelli and cook for 2 to 3 minutes, removing them with slotted spoon.

Serve immediately with a sprinkle of lemon zest and topped with grated cheese.

This can be served on its own as a pasta-style dish or with a ladle of the chicken stock as soup.

Calamari Ripieni
(Stuffed Squid)

Amalia (Eugeni) Fermani, Porto S. Giorgio, Fermo

(Yield: 4 servings)

2 tablespoons (plus extra) extra-virgin olive oil
STUFFING:
½ onion (diced)
2 lbs squid
(cleaned with pouches, tentacles and fins)
½ cup breadcrumbs

¼ cup fresh parsley (chopped fine)
salt and freshly ground pepper

¼ cup breadcrumbs
1 lemon quartered into wedges

1. Warm 2 tablespoons of oil in skillet over medium heat and sauté onions until translucent.

2. Add squid tentacles and fins and cook for approx. 5 minutes. Remove and allow to cool. Coarsely chop tentacles and fins and set aside with onions.

3. Combine breadcrumbs, parsley, chopped squid, onions, salt, pepper and mix in bowl, adding extra oil a little at a time until mixture binds together.

4. Stuff each squid pouch loosely with mixture and close opening using toothpicks. Season with salt and pepper.

5. Grease a baking dish and arrange stuffed pouches in single layer.

6. Sprinkle top of pouches with breadcrumbs and drizzle with extra-virgin olive oil.

7. Cover with aluminum foil and bake in oven preheated to 375°F for 30 minutes.

8. Remove foil and continue baking for another 15 minutes.

9. Garnish plate with fresh parsley and all leftovers from baking dish.

Serve with lemon wedges.

Vincisgrassi
(Lasagna Marche)

Rita Ritucci, Acquabona, Macerata

This signature dish from the region of Marche blends the flavours of the meats used along with a Besciamella sauce. Making the sauce the day before allows the flavours to deepen.

MEAT SAUCE:
2½ ounces prosciutto
(cut into small cubes)
3 tablespoons butter
1 onion (diced)
1 small carrot (diced)
1 cup white wine
salt and freshly ground pepper
½ pound ground beef
½ pound chicken giblets (diced)
¼ pound pork sausage
(casing removed and crumbled)

15 ounces diced tomato
(optional, ¼ pound chicken liver)

~

1 pound lasagna noodles
BESCIAMELLA SAUCE:
2 tablespoons butter
½ cup flour
1½ cups milk (warmed)

~

1 cup grated Parmesan cheese

1. **MEAT SAUCE:** Melt butter in large skillet over medium heat and cook prosciutto for a few minutes. Add onions, carrots, wine, salt and pepper and sauté for a few more minutes. Add beef, giblets, sausage and cook for another 20 minutes. Add tomatoes and (optional) chicken livers along with 6 ounces of water. Cook for another 30 minutes, then remove from heat and set aside.

2. In pot of salted boiling water, cook lasagna strips for approx. 3 minutes, drain and run under cold water to stop cooking process. Allow pasta to drain completely. Put noodles in bowl with a little olive oil so the they will not stick together.

3. Make **BESCIAMELLA SAUCE** as per instructions on page 306 and set aside.

4. Lightly grease lasagna dish and cover with layer of pasta. Spread layers of meat sauce, Besciamella sauce and grated Parmesan cheese. Repeat until all ingredients have been used, ensuring the final layer has meat and Besciamella sauces as well as grated cheese.

5. Bake in oven preheated to 350°F for 20 to 25 minutes or until golden.

Using freshly made pasta, either with or without eggs, is always better and very easy to do. You can find instructions on pages 306-7.

Costolette d'Agnello al Vino
(Lamb Chops with Wine)

Cesira Aiudi, Fossombrone, Pesaro-Urbino

(Yield: 6 servings)

12 lamb chops (seasoned with salt and pepper)
salt and freshly ground pepper
4 tablespoons extra-virgin olive oil
1 teaspoon butter
1 rosemary sprig (minced)
1 cup red wine
SAUCE:
1 teaspoon corn starch
¼ cup water

1. Warm oil and butter in large skillet over medium heat and cook seasoned lamb chops for approx. 3 minutes per side.

2. Lower heat. Add rosemary and wine. Cook for another 6 minutes. Remove lamb chops and place on serving dish.

3. Dissolve corn starch in water. Add starch to skillet and cook remaining juices, stirring until reduced by half.

4. Pour sauce over lamb chops and serve.

Grilled zucchini, peppers and fennel make a great accompaniment.

Brodetto di Pesce
(Fish Soup)

Graziella (Zonea) Bertulli, Fano, Pesaro-Urbino

(Yield: 4 servings)

2 pounds mixed fish
(cuttlefish, calamari, skate, whitefish, turbot, shrimp,
prawn, etc) cleaned and washed
1 garlic clove (minced)
1 small onion (diced)
1 cup white wine

1 5.8 ounce can tomato paste
(diluted in 2 cups water)
1 medium chili pepper (chopped fine)
4 tablespoons white wine vinegar
1 tablespoon finely chopped parsley
extra-virgin olive oil

1. Coat and heat large saucepan with oil over medium heat. Add garlic and onions. Sauté for approx. 1 minute.

2. Add wine, allowing alcohol to evaporate for a few minutes, then add diluted tomato paste and bring to boil.

3. Add cuttlefish and squid with pinch of chili and cook 5 to 6 minutes. Add remaining fish and cook for 3 additional minutes. Add shrimp and prawns last. Cook for another 2 minutes.

4. Add vinegar and parsley. Cook for another 2 minutes.

5. Remove from heat and allow to sit for 2-3 minutes.

Serve with toasted slices of pane casareccio or focaccia.

If you wish, mussels and clams can be added. If soup is too thick while cooking, add a little extra water.

Pasticciata
(Slow Cooked Eye of Round)

Emilia (Giuliani) Vagnini, Fano, Pesaro-Urbino

(Yield: 8 servings)

4 pounds eye of round (beef)

3 slices pancetta (diced)

1 medium onion (diced)

5 cloves

2 garlic cloves (minced)

6 ounces white wine

1 teaspoon each, salt and pepper

water

1. In large Dutch oven over medium heat, cook pancetta for approx. 3 minutes. Add eye of round and braise until browned on all sides.

2. Add onions, cloves, garlic, wine, salt and pepper. Cook for approx. 6 minutes.

3. Add enough water to cover meat half-way. Add salt and pepper. Cook partially covered for approx. 2 hours.

4. Remove meat from Dutch oven and allow to cool until reaching room temperature.

5. Cut meat in slices, allowing juices to flow for a few minutes.

6. Return sliced meat back to pot over medium heat. Include all juices. Continue cooking for 1 more hour.

Serve with roasted or mashed potatoes, topped with cooking sauce.

Stoccafisso alla Marchigiana
(Salted Dry Cod)

Ida (Catá) Eugeni, Porto S. Giorgio, Fermo

The use of bay leaves gives the Stoccafisso a wonderful flavour. The more you add the better it tastes.

(Yield: 4 servings)

2½ pounds stoccafisso/baccalà (dry salted cod)
3 tablespoons (plus extra) extra-virgin olive oil
24+ bay leaves (to taste)
salt and freshly ground pepper

1 tablespoon finely chopped parsley
2 garlic cloves (minced)
1 cup white wine

1. Prep cod as on page 306.
2. Using kitchen mallet, lightly pound cod flat.
3. Cut cod into 3-inch fillets.
4. Spread oil in large baking dish and cover bottom with bed of bay leaves.
5. Place cod pieces on top of bay leaves. Sprinkle with salt, pepper, parsley and garlic.
6. Pour wine over dish and sprinkle with extra-virgin olive oil.
7. Bake on middle rack in oven preheated to 350°F for 1 hour.
8. Plate stoccafisso, adding some of remaining cooking liquid on top.

Serve immediately.

Tagliatelle con Pesce alla Marchigiana
(Tagliatelle with Fish)

Amalia (Eugeni) Fermani, Porto S. Giorgio, Fermo

The fish for this recipe is a little difficult to get but not impossible. We have found excellent substitutes that do justice to this dish, (as shown in the ingredients list in brackets).

(Yield: 4 servings)

1 pound tagliatelle pasta
2 Triglie (Red Mullet)
2 Busbane or Zanchette (Sea Bass)
2 Sogliole (Sole or Tilapia)
2 Minnole (Grouper)
2 tablespoons extra-virgin olive oil

2 tablespoons tomato paste
½ cup water
1 fresh chili (chopped fine)
1 teaspoon each salt and freshly ground pepper
1 tablespoon parsley (chopped fine)

1. Clean all fish and remove innards but leave skin on. Grill over medium heat for approx. 3 minutes per side. Remove skin, bone, tail and head. Set aside.

2. Warm oil in large skillet over medium heat. Add tomato paste, water and chili. Salt and pepper to taste, and stir.

3. Add fish fillets and cook for 10 minutes. Remove from heat. Add parsley.

4. Meanwhile, in large pot of salted boiling water, cook pasta until al dente. Drain and add to saucepan with fish fillets and cook for another minute. Mix well.

Serve hot and garnish with fresh parsley.

Risotto ai Gamberi
(Risotto and Shrimp)

Emilio Eugeni, Porto S. Giorgio, Fermo

(Yield: 4 servings)

4 teaspoons extra-virgin olive oil
1 onion (diced)
½ pound small shrimp (shelled and deveined)
2 cups rice

6 cups vegetable broth (hot)
1 tablespoon curry
Parmigiano-Reggiano

1. Warm oil in large skillet over medium heat and sauté onions until translucent.

2. Add shrimp and stir well.

3. Add rice and enough broth to cover mixture, stirring continuously.

4. As broth gets absorbed, continue adding more one ladle at a time.

5. When rice is almost al dente (the broth should be all used up) add curry and continue stirring until slightly creamy.

6. Remove from heat. Add handful of cheese (to taste). Mix and serve.

Serve hot.

Vitello Ubriaco
(Veal Steak in Wine)

Cesira Aiudi, Fossombrone, Pesaro-Urbino

(Yield: 4 servings)

4 1-inch veal steaks (sirloin or strip loin)
salt and freshly ground pepper
4 tablespoons extra-virgin olive oil
SAUCE:
2 large shallots (thinly sliced)
3 cups red wine
1 tablespoon tomato paste
1 garlic clove (minced)
1 teaspoon finely chopped parsley

1. Season each steak with salt and pepper on both sides.

2. Warm 3 tablespoons of oil in large skillet over medium-high heat and cook steaks to your liking (rare, medium or well-done). Once cooked, remove steaks from pan and allow to sit covered with foil.

3. Warm remaining oil in same pan over medium heat. Sauté shallots for approx. 3 minutes, then add wine and continue cooking until alcohol has evaporated.

4. Add tomato paste and stir well. Add garlic and parsley. Continue cooking for approx. 3 minutes.

Pour sauce over steaks and serve immediately.

UMBRIA

CAPITAL

Perugia

RED WINE

Sagrantino

WHITE WINE

Orvieto Bianco

Baccalà con Patate
(Salted Cod with Potatoes)

Gina Marcelloni, Bovara di Trevi, Perugia

(Yield: 4 servings)

1 pound baccalà
½ cup extra-virgin olive oil
2 onions (diced)
5 garlic cloves (minced)

5 cups tomatoes (diced) or 28 oz can
salt and freshly ground pepper
3 potatoes (sliced ¼-inch)

1. Prepare baccalà as per instructions on page 306 and cut into large pieces.

2. Warm oil in large saucepan over medium heat. Add onions and garlic and cook until onions are caramelized (golden).

3. Add tomatoes. Salt and pepper to taste. Bring to boil and cook for approx. 3 minutes.

4. Add potatoes, ensuring that all potatoes are covered. If they are not, add water. Allow mixture to return to boil. Cook until potatoes are tender. Add baccalà pieces, reduce heat to simmer and cook partially covered for 45 to 60 minutes.

Serve immediately.

Carciofini Fritti
(Fried Baby Artichokes)

Letizia (Marcelloni) Micheli, Bovara di Trevi, Perugia

(Yield: 4 servings)

6 baby artichokes	**8 tablespoons flour**
2 lemons (quartered)	**6 eggs (beaten)**
canola oil	

1. Cut 1 inch from tops of artichokes, remove outer leaves and halve lengthwise. Soak in cold water with half the lemons for approx. 1 hour.

2. In pot of boiling water, blanch artichoke halves (approx. 5 minutes, until semi-soft) and remove with slotted spoon. Place on clean kitchen towel and allow to dry and cool to room temperature.

3. Warm medium-size saucepan with approx. 2 inches of oil over medium heat.

4. Meanwhile, combine flour and eggs in bowl and beat until heavy-cream mixture is obtained.

5. Dip artichoke halves in cream-mixture and then carefully place in heated oil.

6. Fry artichoke halves until golden brown, then remove with slotted spoon and place on plate with paper towels.

Sprinkle with salt and serve as appetizer or first course.

Peperonata di Coniglio
(Rabbit with Stewed Vegetables)

Franco Marcelloni, Bovara di Trevi, Perugia

(Yield: 4 servings)

½ cup extra-virgin olive oil
4 garlic cloves (chopped)
1 onion (diced)
1 whole rabbit
(3 lbs, cut into 12 ¼-pound pieces)
salt and freshly ground pepper
1 teaspoon chili flakes
1 tablespoon fresh rosemary (chopped)

½ lemon
1 cup white wine
3 peppers (green, red and orange)
cut in ½-inch strips
½ cup parsley (chopped fine)
4 cups crushed or diced tomatoes
5.5 ounces tomato paste (1 can)

1. Warm oil in large saucepan over medium heat. Add garlic and onions and sauté for approx. 3 minutes.

2. Add rabbit pieces. Season with salt, pepper, chili flakes and rosemary. Cook 15 to 20 minutes, turning rabbit pieces until slightly brown.

3. Add wine and juice from half the lemon. Continue cooking for another 5 minutes.

4. Add peppers and parsley and cover. Continue cooking for another 30 minutes.

5. Add tomatoes and tomato paste, mix well, cover and cook for another hour.

   You can serve this rabbit, which literally falls off the bone, over your favourite pasta, rice, or on its own.

Fegatelli
(Pork Liver with Bacon)

Oliviero Marcelloni, Bovara di Trevi, Perugia

(Yield: 4 servings)

1½ pounds pork liver (cut 2-inch cubes)
salt and freshly ground pepper
chilies (optional)
12+ bay leaves
¼ pound pancetta (¼-inch thick, cut in 2-inch squares)

For the BBQ or Grill:

1. Put liver in bowl and season with salt, pepper and (optional) chilies. Marinate for approx. 15 minutes.

2. Add piece of liver, bay leaf and piece of pancetta to skewer. Repeat process until skewers are filled.

3. With BBQ or grill on low heat, cook for approx. 20 to 30 minutes.

Note: using ½-pound ratta di maiale (netting from pig), each skewer can be wrapped tightly and then cooked in the same manner.

Gobbi al Forno
(Baked Artichoke Stems)

Gina (Chiariotti) Marcelloni, Bovara di Trevi, Perugia

(Yield: 4 servings)

12 Gobbi (artichoke stems)
¼ cup flour
1 tablespoon extra-virgin olive oil
2 tablespoons butter (¼-inch bits)

¼ cup Parmesan cheese
2 teaspoons red chili flakes
4 cups tomato sauce

1. Cut gobbies approx. 3 inches long.

2. In pot of boiling water, blanch gobbies for approx. 3 minutes. Remove and pat dry.

3. Add flour to bowl, then dredge gobbies until fully coated.

4. Lightly oil 6x6 baking dish and place gobbies in layer.

5. Put a few pats of butter on top of gobbies. Sprinkle with cheese and chili flakes, then cover with tomato sauce. *If using more gobbies, continue building layers as above.*

6. Bake in oven preheated to 350°F for between 1 and 1½ hours.

Gobbies are the edible extensions of the artichoke heart. Depending on how young they are, you may or may not want to peel them. With the younger stems it is not necessary, but when using older stems, peeling will bring out their softness.

Carciofini Fritti
(Deep-fried Baby Artichokes)

Letizia (Marcelloni) Micheli, Bovara di Trevi, Perugia

(Yield: 4 servings)

12 baby artichokes
1 lemon (quartered and juiced)
2 eggs
1 cup flour

1. Cut approx. ½ inch from tops of artichokes and remove rough outer layer of leaves.

2. Put cut and cleaned artichokes in large pot of cold water with lemons and lemon juice and allow to stand for approx. 10 minutes.

3. Place pot over medium heat and allow to boil for 20 to 30 minutes.

4. Drain artichokes and allow to dry completely (stand them upside down to drain).

5. While artichokes are draining, whisk eggs in bowl until fluffy. Add flour and mix until pancake-like.

6. Dip artichokes in mixture and place in deep fryer until golden.

Serve warm with your favourite dipping sauce.

If a deep fryer is not available, heat a medium-sized saucepan with enough canola oil (approx. 2 inches deep) to deep-fry the artichokes. Special care should be used when inserting or removing the artichokes from the hot oil (a spider works well).

Lasagna con Besciamella
(Lasagna with Besciamella Sauce)

Graziella Marcelloni, Bovara di Trevi, Perugia

(Yield: 6 servings)

2 pounds lasagna noodles
1 tablespoon extra-virgin olive oil
4 cups besciamella sauce (as per instructions on page 306) with 1 tablespoon tomato sauce

4 cups meat sauce (your favourite recipe)
¼ pound each Parmigiano-Reggiano and Romano cheeses (mixed)
1½ pounds Mozzarella (grated)

1. In large pot of salted boiling water, add 1 tablespoon of olive oil. Cook lasagna noodles for approx. 4 to 5 minutes.

2. Drain and run cold water over noodles to stop cooking process. Place in bowl, drizzle with olive oil and toss.

3. Line bottom of 9x12 baking dish with thin layer of meat sauce.

4. Place layer of lasagna noodles on bottom of dish. Add layer of meat sauce, layer of mixed Parmigiano and Romano, and a good sprinkle of Mozzarella. Finish with layer of besciamella sauce. Repeat process until all ingredients have been used. *The last layer should be that of besciamella, with meat sauce on top.*

5. Bake covered in aluminum foil in oven preheated to 350°F for 2 hours. In final 10 minutes, remove foil and broil until top is light golden.

Pomodori Ripieni
(Stuffed Tomatoes)

Paolina (Bonpadre) Chiariotti, Borgo di Trevi, Perugia

(Yield: 4 servings)

4 tomatoes (ripe and firm)
½ tablespoon chili flakes
8 garlic cloves (minced)
¼ cup finely chopped Italian parsley

1½ cups breadcrumbs
1 tablespoon salt
1 teaspoon pepper
2 tablespoons extra-virgin olive oil (plus extra)

1. Cut each tomato in half, removing and reserving pulp in a bowl.

2. Add chili flakes, garlic, parsley, breadcrumbs, salt, pepper, and olive oil to tomato pulp. Mix well.

3. To test filling, take a handful and gently squeeze and release. If it remains together, mixture is well-set: if not, add a little more olive oil.

4. Stuff each tomato half with mixture, giving it a light press as you fill.

5. Place stuffed tomatoes in lightly greased oven dish and bake in oven preheated to 350°F for 30 minutes.

Remove, drizzle with oil and serve immediately.

Amounts for the ingredients are approximate and based on medium-large tomatoes. Unseasoned breadcrumbs should be used because they are the main ingredient for the filling.

Gnocchi di Patate
(Potato Gnocchi)

Gina (Chiariotti) Marcelloni, Bovara di Trevi, Perugia

(Yield: 4 servings)

5 cups mashed potatoes
1 egg (beaten)
salt and freshly ground pepper
flour

1. In bowl combine room-temperature mashed potatoes and beaten egg. Salt and pepper to taste.

2. Add flour one tablespoon at a time, mixing until dough-like and manageable.

3. Cut piece of dough and roll, on slightly floured surface, into ½-inch-thick log. Cut log into 1-inch pieces and set aside on lightly floured cookie sheet. Continue until all dough has been used.

4. Bring large pot of salted water to boil, and add one layer of gnocchi. Cook until risen to surface.

5. Remove with spider and set aside. Continue until all gnocchi have been cooked.

Serve gnocchi with tomato sauce (see page 308) and top with freshly grated Pecorino or Romano cheese.

As an alternative, try using sweet potatoes.

Pasta alla Aragosta
(Pasta with Lobster Claws)

Teresa (Santomo Stornelli) Medei, Bovara di Trevi, Perugia

(Yield: 4 servings)

3 pounds lobster claws (with arms)
½ cup extra-virgin olive oil
3 garlic cloves (minced)
½ teaspoon chili flakes
¼ cup finely chopped parsley

8 cups diced tomatoes
4 cups water
salt and freshly ground pepper
1 pound pasta (linguini/spaghetti)

1. Warm oil in large saucepan over medium heat. Add garlic, chili flakes and parsley and cook for approx. 1 minute.

2. Add tomatoes and water. Season with salt and pepper. Once boiling, reduce heat to simmer and cook partially covered for approx. 1 hour.

3. While sauce is cooking, bring large pot of salted water to boil. Add lobster and cook for approx. 3 minutes. Remove lobster and set aside.

4. Add pasta to lobster pot and cook until al dente.

5. Add lobster to sauce as pasta nears completion. Cook briefly until lobster is reheated.

6. Drain pasta and add to saucepan. Mix together, cooking for approx. 1 minute.

Serve immediately.

Lobster claws should be partially split before cooking, making them easier to eat.

LAZIO

CAPITAL
Roma

RED WINE
Castelli Romani

WHITE WINE
Colli Albani

Fagioli con le Cotiche
(Beans with Pork Skin)

Renato Chechi, Roma

(Yield: 4 servings)

2 pounds dry Romano beans
2 pounds pork skin (cleaned)
3 tablespoons extra-virgin olive oil
1 onion (diced)

1 teaspoon chili flakes
4 cups tomato sauce
salt and freshly ground pepper
¼ cup grated Romano and Parmigiano cheese

1. Bring large pot of salted water to boil. Add Romano beans and cook between 1 and 1½ hours, until tender.

2. Remove beans with spider, set aside and reserve cooking liquid.

3. In same pot, add pork skins and cook for approx. 15 minutes or until tender. Remove and set aside.

4. Warm oil in large skillet over medium heat. Add onions, chili flakes, tomato sauce and a pinch of salt and pepper. Cook between 5 and 7 minutes.

5. Add beans and pork skins. Once boiling, reduce to simmer and cook for 20 minutes.

Remove from heat, sprinkle with cheeses and serve warm.

Linguine Cacio e Pepe
(Linguine with Cheese and Pepper)

Sora Ida, Ciampino, Roma

(Yield: 4 servings)

1 pound linguine	½ tablespoon black pepper
1 cup Romano cheese	3 tablespoons tomato sauce
1 cup Ricotta cheese	1 teaspoon salt
1 cup Parmigiano-Reggiano cheese	

1. Cook pasta in large pot of salted water until al dente.

2. Meanwhile, mix 3 cheeses in bowl. Add black pepper and mix, then add tomato sauce and salt and re-mix.

3. Once pasta is al dente, drain, reserving 1 cup of cooking liquid.

4. Add cooking liquid ½ cup at a time to cheese mixture until sauce is creamy and pink. Add sauce to pasta and toss thoroughly.

Serve immediately, topped with Parmesan cheese.

Trippa alla Romana
(Tripe Roman Style)

Mario Colasanti, Roma

(Yield: 6 servings)

2 pounds tripe
3 tablespoons extra-virgin olive oil
1 red onion (sliced thinly)
4 garlic cloves (minced)

salt and freshly ground pepper
2 cups tomato sauce
¼ cup freshly grated Pecorino
¼ cup freshly grated Parmesan

1. Place tripe in large pot and cover with water by 2 inches. Bring to boil and cook until tripe is very tender (approx. 1 hour).

2. Drain tripe, cool and slice into 1-inch strips.

3. Warm oil in large skillet over high heat. Add onions, garlic and tripe strips. Season with salt and pepper. Cook for approx. 5 minutes.

4. Add tomato sauce. Once boiling, reduce to medium heat, cover and cook for 30 minutes.

5. Remove from heat. Add half of cheeses and mix well.

Serve in individual bowls or plates topped with remaining cheeses.

Gnocchi di Semolino alla Romana
(Gnocchi with Semolina Flour)

Mario Chechi, Roma

(Yield: 4 servings)

4 cups of milk
½ teaspoon salt
1½ cups Semolina flour
2 egg yolks (beaten)

¾ cup grated Parmigiano cheese
extra-virgin olive oil
7 tablespoons butter (melted)
salt and freshly ground pepper

1. Warm milk and salt in pot over medium heat. Once boiling, add semolina flour and stir continuously until thickened, making sure to avoid lumps.

2. Remove from heat. Add egg yolks with ½ cup of Parmigiano cheese. Stir until blended. Set aside.

3. Lightly grease cookie tray and evenly pour mixture into it (approx. ½-inch thick). Allow to cool completely.

4. Using butter, grease a 9x12 oven dish.

5. Once semolina mixture is cooled, use glass or 3-inch round cookie cutter to cut out discs. Place in greased dish, slightly overlapping.

6. Cover discs with remaining cheese and butter. Season with salt and pepper.

7. Bake in oven preheated to 350°F for approx. 25 minutes or until a golden crust forms on top.

Serve hot or at room temperature.

Coda di Vitello alla Vaccinara
(Oxtail)

Alberto Colantoni, Roma

(Yield: 4 servings)

1 pound oxtail
5 tablespoons extra-virgin olive oil
1 celery stalk (diced)
1 onion (diced)
1 carrot (diced)

1 teaspoon salt
1 teaspoon chili pepper
½ cup white wine
4 cups tomato sauce
3 cups beef broth

1. Rinse oxtail under cold water, pat dry and cut into 8 pieces.

2. Warm oil in large saucepan over medium heat. Brown oxtail pieces.

3. Add all diced vegetables, salt, and chili peppers. Cook, stirring occasionally for approx. 5 minutes.

4. Add wine and continue to stir until alcohol has evaporated. Add tomato sauce and 2 cups of broth. Stir again.

5. Once boiling, reduce to simmer and cook covered for approx. 2½ hours. Stir occasionally and add broth as needed to keep mixture moist.

Serve with rice or polenta.

Carciofi alla Romana
(Artichokes Roman Style)

Anna Maria (Chechi) Innocente, Roma

(Yield: 4 servings)

4 artichokes
STUFFING:
2 tablespoons finely chopped fresh parsley
1 tablespoon finely chopped fresh mint
2 garlic cloves (minced)
salt, to taste

freshly ground pepper, to taste
1 tablespoon extra-virgin olive oil

1 cup boiling water
½ cup white wine
1 cup extra-virgin olive oil

1. In small bowl combine parsley, mint, garlic, salt, pepper, and 1 tablespoon olive oil. Set aside.
2. Remove tough outer layer of leaves and cut off approx. 1 inch from top. Cut bottom to sit flat.
3. Remove choke and fill with stuffing.
4. Arrange artichokes closely together in small pot. Ensure they stay closed!
5. Add boiling water, wine, 1 cup olive oil and a pinch of salt. Cover with lid and cook over low heat until all water has evaporated.

Serve seasoned with salt and freshly ground pepper.

When choosing artichokes for this recipe, try to select a medium size. Larger ones can be used but because they are tougher more water and wine will be needed when cooking. When cutting the bottom, if the stalks are long, reserve and use them for the Gobbi recipe found on page 168.

Linguine alle Nocciole e Rughetta
(Linguine with Hazelnuts and Arugula)

Silvana Pellegrini, Pontecorvo, Frosinone

(Yield: 2 servings)

1 tablespoon extra-virgin olive oil
½ cup chopped hazelnuts
salt and freshly ground pepper (to taste)
½ cup chicken broth
½ pound linguine
1 bunch arugula (chopped rough)
¼ cup grated Parmesan cheese

1. Warm oil in saucepan over medium heat. Add hazelnuts and pinch of salt. Toast, making sure not to burn (approx. 3 minutes).

2. Add broth and continue to cook until reduced by half. Set aside.

3. While toasting hazelnuts, add linguine to large pot of salted boiling water and cook until al dente.

4. Drain cooked pasta and toss with arugula, hazelnut mixture and cheese.

Serve hot.

Peperoni di Magro
(Stuffed Peppers without Meat)

Silvana Pellegrini, Pontecorvo, Frosinone

(Yield: 4 servings)

2 red peppers
2 yellow peppers
STUFFING:
1 tablespoon olive oil
1 onion (diced)
7 anchovy fillets in oil (cut in small pieces)

1 cup chopped walnuts
2 tablespoons finely chopped parsley
2 tablespoons grated parmesan cheese
2 tablespoons breadcrumbs
salt and freshly ground pepper

1/3 cup extra-virgin olive oil

1. Wash and dry peppers. Cut in half, remove seeds and pith and set aside.

2. Warm 1 tablespoon of oil in skillet over medium heat. Add onions and anchovies, cooking until onions turn light brown.

3. Pour cooked mixture into bowl and add walnuts, parsley, Parmesan cheese, breadcrumbs, salt and pepper. Mix well and stuff pepper halves equally.

4. Grease medium-size baking dish and add stuffed pepper halves side by side. Cover with aluminum foil and bake in oven preheated to 450°F for approx. 20 minutes.

5. Remove foil. Sprinkle peppers with remaining olive oil and bake for another 15 minutes.

Serve hot or at room temperature.

Coratella con Carciofi
(Lamb Innards with Artichokes)

Maria (Fusaro) Colasanti, Roma

(Yield: 4 servings)

1½ pounds assorted lamb innards (heart, liver, lungs, spleen,
kidneys, and intestines. Note: these are normally sold together.)

6 baby artichokes

4 tablespoons extra-virgin olive oil

1 onion (diced)

2 garlic cloves (minced)

1 red chili (or more to taste)

8 sage leaves

1 sprig rosemary (leaves only)

1 bay leaf

½ cup white wine

salt

1. Clean and slice all innards into ¾-inch cubes and set aside.

2. Clean and remove choke and outer leaves of artichokes. Cut into thin strips and set aside.

3. Warm oil in large skillet over medium heat and sauté onions, garlic and chilies for approx. 5 minutes.

4. Add lamb innards and continue cooking for another 15 minutes.

5. Reduce heat to low, add sage, rosemary, bay leaves, artichoke strips, a pinch of salt and wine. Cook for another 20 minutes, stirring occasionally.

When ready to serve, remove bay leaf.

Frittata di Asparagi
(Asparagus Omelette)

Domenico Aversa, Ceccano, Frosinone

Memories of my youth came flooding back as I read about the opening of Caboto Park in the month of May. The long ride down Howard Avenue, then onto Gore Road in Harrow, always involved a mandatory stop along the side of the road to pick the wild asparagus which grew along the sides of the ditches. My father Carlo was the ultimate "gatherer" and spring was asparagus and wild mushroom season. Of course, mother Vittoria then turned the ingredients into a culinary delight. This simple dish pays homage to them.

(Yield: 4 servings)

2 teaspoons extra-virgin olive oil
1 onion (thinly sliced)
12 asparagus spears (tough ends removed and cut diagonally into 1-inch lengths)

½ teaspoon salt
½ teaspoon freshly ground pepper
6 eggs (lightly beaten)

1. Warm oil in large non-stick skillet over medium-high heat. Add onions and sauté until translucent.

2. Add asparagus, salt, and pepper and reduce heat to medium-low, cooking covered until tender (approx. 6 to 8 minutes).

3. Pour in eggs and cook until almost set, but slightly runny on top (approx. 2 to 4 minutes).

4. Cover and continue cooking until top is set (or flip and cook until bottom is golden).

Cut into wedges and serve immediately.

Pomodori col Riso
(Tomatoes Stuffed with Rice)

Mafalda (Colasanti) Chechi, Grottaferrata, Roma

(Yield: 4 servings)

4 large firm tomatoes
3 tablespoons extra-virgin olive oil
6 tablespoons long grain rice

1 tablespoon salt
1 tablespoon pepper
extra-virgin olive oil

1. Cut tops off tomatoes approx. ½ inch down and set aside. Hollow and reserve all contents in a bowl.

2. Break reserved tomatoes into small pieces. Add oil, rice, salt and pepper and mix well. Season to personal taste. Allow to sit covered in refrigerator for 30 to 45 minutes.

3. Fill chilled hollowed tomatoes with mixture. Reserve whatever mixture is leftover.

4. Place cut tops back onto tomatoes to seal.

5. Lightly oil a deep 8x11 dish or small roasting pan and place tomatoes in centre, about ½ inch apart.

6. Pour remaining mixture between and around tomatoes and lightly drizzle with olive oil.

7. Bake in oven preheated to 450°F for approx. 1½ hours.

Once rice in mixture has turned slightly brown, remove and serve.

Cubed potatoes can be added around the tomatoes while cooking.

Rapini Saltati
(Rapini)

Brigida Califano, Ponza, Latina

Rapini is a common ingredient in southern Italian cuisines. A vegetable with many spiked leaves that surround clusters of green buds that resemble small heads of broccoli, small, edible yellow flowers may also be found blooming among the buds. The flavour of rapini has been described as nutty, bitter, and pungent.

(Yield: 4 servings)

1 pound rapini
1 tablespoon extra-virgin olive oil
1 garlic clove (sliced thin)
1 teaspoon chili flakes
salt

1. Bring pot of salted water to boil. Add rapini and cook for approx. 5 minutes.

2. Drain in colander and set aside.

3. Warm oil in skillet over medium heat. Sauté garlic until fragrant and lightly browned.

4. Add rapini and chili flakes and cook for 10 to 15 minutes.

Serve immediately.

Pasta Carbonara alla Romana
(Pasta with Pancetta and Eggs)

Mauro Chechi, Roma

Although this dish has many variations, this is a true Roman version that is not only wonderful but simple to make.

(Yield: 4 servings)

1 pound spaghetti (or your favourite long pasta)
3 large eggs
1 teaspoon salt
4 teaspoons black pepper (or more)

2 tablespoons extra-virgin olive oil
3 garlic cloves (minced)
4 ounces pancetta
(sliced 1/8-inch thick and diced)

1. Bring large pot of salted water to boil. Add pasta and cook until al dente.

2. While pasta is cooking, whisk eggs in bowl until fluffy. Add salt and pepper and continue to whisk until well-blended.

3. Working quickly, as pasta approaches al dente, heat oil in large skillet over medium heat. Add garlic and pancetta and cook until garlic is lightly browned but not burnt.

4. Drain pasta and add to skillet. Toss, cooking for another minute.

5. Turn off heat and wait 1 minute. Add egg mixture and mix until saucy. Cover for approx. 1 minute.

Re-season to taste and serve immediately.

ABRUZZO

CAPITAL
L'Aquila

RED WINE
Montepulciano d'Abruzzo

WHITE WINE
Trebbiano d'Abruzzo

Maccheroni con Zucchine (Aquilana)
(Macaroni with Zucchini and Saffron)

Lucia (Duronio) Cutrone, Prata D'Ansidonia, L'Aquila

(Yield: 4 servings)

ZUCCHINI SAUCE:

4 cups extra-virgin olive oil
1 cup onion (diced)
3 cups hot water
5 small zucchini, 1½ pounds
(cut to matchsticks 2 inches long)
1 cup finely chopped scallions

2 teaspoons salt
¼ teaspoon saffron threads
(toasted and steeped*)
2 tablespoons Italian parsley (finely chopped)

1 pound macaroni
2 large egg yolks
1 cup grated Pecorino cheese

1. Bring large pot of salted water to boil.

2. While water is boiling, heat oil in large skillet over medium heat and sauté onions until translucent.

3. Add ½ cup hot water and cook for 2 minutes.

4. Increase heat to high. Add zucchini, scallions and salt. Once boiling, cook for another 2 minutes.

5. Add 2 more cups of hot water, saffron with infused water,* and chopped parsley.

6. Allow to boil then lower heat to simmer.

7. Add pasta to boiling water and cook until al dente.

8. While waiting for pasta to cook, whisk egg yolks in a bowl, slowly adding last ½ cup of hot water to thin and temper yolks.

9. When the pasta is cooked, drain and add to zucchini sauce. Toss pasta quickly and remove from heat.

10. While continuing to toss, pour egg mixture over pasta, allowing eggs to cook with the residual heat.

Sprinkle with cheese, toss again and serve immediately, topped with more cheese.

*Toasting/steeping saffron: Place saffron strands in a metal spoon. Hold spoon over low open flame for a few seconds, toasting threads very gently. This will bring out the scent of the threads more fully. Immediately put the threads into a small dish with 2 tablespoons of hot water and allow to steep for approx. 15 minutes.

Spaghettini con Acciughe
(Spaghettini with Anchovy Sauce)

Alba (Cence) Di Padova, San Donato, Frosinone

(Yield: 4 servings)

½ pound spaghettini (thin spaghetti)
½ cup extra-virgin olive oil
¼ cup butter
2 garlic cloves (minced)
2 ounces anchovy fillets
3 tablespoons fresh parsley (chopped fine)

1. Cook spaghettini in large pot of *unsalted* water until al dente.

2. While pasta is cooking, heat oil and butter in skillet over medium heat. Add garlic and anchovies and stir. Make sure to mash anchovies, and cook for approx. 5 minutes or until anchovies have completely blended.

3. Drain pasta and add to skillet. Add parsley and toss, ensuring pasta is evenly coated.

Serve immediately.
Spaghettini is thinner spaghetti pasta.

Agnello alle Olive
(Lamb Chops with Olives)

Tonino Duronio, Prata D'Ansidonia, L'Aquila

(Yield: 6 servings)

6 lamb loin chops
(bone-in, 1½ inches thick)
1 teaspoon kosher salt
¼ cup all-purpose flour
2 tablespoons extra-virgin olive oil
5 garlic cloves (peeled and crushed)

1 lemon, juiced (2 tablespoons)
½ cup water
1 cup black olives (pitted)
1 teaspoon dried oregano
¼ teaspoon chili flakes
(or to taste)

1. Salt chops lightly all over, using ½ teaspoon salt.

2. Dredge chops with flour on both sides, shaking off excess.

3. Warm oil slowly in large skillet over medium-low heat.

4. Lay chops in skillet (they should fit snugly in one layer). Cook for 3 minutes or until lightly browned, then turn over and repeat.

5. Add crushed garlic cloves in spaces between chops. Allow chops to sizzle and caramelize, turning garlic as they darken. Do not burn.

6. Turn chops, giving both sides another 2 to 3 minutes of browning (total: 10 minutes).

7. Pour lemon juice and water around chops and sprinkle with remaining salt.

8. When liquid begins to bubble, drop olives around chops and shake skillet to distribute.

9. Sprinkle oregano and chili flakes, lower heat to simmer and cook covered.

10. Turn chops until juices have thickened and adhere to meat like a moist glaze (approx. 10 minutes).

11. Turn off heat and let chops sit for a couple of minutes in skillet to absorb moisture.

12. Serve directly from skillet, with olives and pan juices spooned over the chops.

Baccalà con Patate
(Salted Cod with Potatoes)

Adalberto Di Padova, Windsor, Ontario

(Yield: 4 servings)

2½ pounds baccalà

3 tablespoons extra-virgin olive oil

1 onion (diced)

5 potatoes (cubed 1½-inch)

2 tomatoes (peeled and diced)

3 cups of water

1. Once baccalà has been prepared as per instructions on page 306, cut into 8 even pieces.

2. Warm oil in large saucepan over medium heat. Add baccalà, onions, potatoes, tomatoes and water. Cook covered for approx. 30 minutes or until sauce has thickened.

Serve the baccalà while hot, topped with thickened sauce.

Ravioli Ripieni con Ricotta
(Ricotta-filled Ravioli)

Irma (Giansante) Colarossi, Carpineto della Nora, Pescara

(Yield: 4 servings)

PASTA DOUGH:
4 cups flour (extra for dusting)
1 cup water
4 eggs

FILLING:
1 egg
1 pound Ricotta cheese (drained)
¾ cup grated Romano cheese
¼ cup finely chopped Italian parsley
1 teaspoon each, salt and freshly ground pepper

1. Prepare dough as per pages 306-7.

2. For filling, combine egg, Ricotta, Romano cheese, parsley, salt and pepper in bowl. Mix well.

3. Refrigerate wrapped for approx. an hour (or overnight).

4. When assembling, divide dough into 4 sections.

5. Working with one section at a time, roll out dough with rolling pin into long sheet, 6 inches wide and approx. 1/8-inch thick. Make sure to flour your surface so dough does not stick.

6. Drop rounded teaspoons of filling onto centre of rolled-out dough (approx. 2 inches apart).

7. Fold dough lengthwise over filling, top to bottom, and press firmly along edges. Then press dough in between fillings, sealing together.

8. Position ravioli cutter between lumps of filling and slice. Continue until pasta is entirely cut.

9. Place ravioli on a floured baking sheet or floured surface (covered). Repeat from step #5 until all ingredients are used.

10. In large pot of boiling salted water, drop in ravioli and cook for approx. 5 minutes. Test one ravioli to ensure Ricotta filling is cooked. Remove with a slotted spoon and serve with your favourite sauce.

For this recipe we browned some sage leaves in butter until crisp and added edible florets from the sage plant as a garnish.

Arrosto di Agnello
(Roast Leg of Lamb)

Domenico Di Padova, Pescocostanzo, L'Aquila

(Yield: 6 servings)

5 pound leg of lamb
2 tablespoons extra-virgin olive oil
4 garlic cloves (each cut into ¼ length pieces)
zest of 1 lemon

½ teaspoon crushed black pepper
1 teaspoon salt
½ teaspoon rosemary (minced)

1. Wipe leg of lamb with clean damp cloth and brush with olive oil.

2. Using sharp knife, make sliver cuts throughout leg and insert ¼-cloves of garlic in all openings.

3. Rub zest over leg, inserting some into slivered cuts.

5. Combine pepper, salt and rosemary. Sprinkle.

6. Using shallow roasting pan with rack, roast in oven preheated to 300°F for approx. 4 hours (until golden).

7. Remove and place on cutting board with fatty side up and slice.

Serve with roasted potatoes and your favourite vegetables.

Melanzane alla Parmigiana
(Eggplant Parmesan)

Marta Di Giallonardo, Cansano, L'Aquila

(Yield: 4 servings)

1 large eggplant (cut crosswise ½-inch thick)
½ cup extra-virgin olive oil
12 ounces crushed tomatoes
2 tablespoons tomato paste
salt and freshly ground pepper (to taste)

2 cups breadcrumbs
½ cup grated Parmesan cheese
½ cup parsley (chopped fine)
2 garlic cloves (minced)
½ pound Mozzarella cheese

1. Warm 2 tablespoons of oil in large skillet over low heat. Add tomatoes, paste, a pinch of salt and pepper. Stir until well mixed. Allow to simmer for approx. 30 minutes and set aside in bowl.

2. Place sliced eggplants in another bowl and cover with hot water. Allow to stand for approx. 5 minutes. Drain and pat dry.

3. Using the same skillet, heat remaining oil over medium heat and fry eggplant slices for approx. 3 minutes on each side, or until tender but still firm. Sprinkle with salt and pepper on each side. Remove from pan and place on paper towels to absorb excess oil.

4. Combine breadcrumbs, cheese, parsley, garlic, a pinch of salt and pepper in bowl. Set aside.

5. Lightly grease bottom of a 6x6 baking dish and cover with layer of eggplant. Sprinkle with breadcrumb mixture, spread with tomato sauce and continue to layer until all ingredients have been used.

6. Layer top with thinly cut Mozzarella cheese and bake in oven preheated to 350°F for approx. 10 minutes, or until the Mozzarella turns golden.

Serve hot.

Pasta e Ceci
(Pasta and Chickpeas)

Marta Di Padova, Pescocostanzo, L'Aquila

(Yield: 4 servings)

½ pound tubetti pasta (or any short style)

1½ cups chickpeas (pre-cooked in a can)

extra-virgin olive oil

2 garlic cloves (slivered)

salt and freshly ground pepper (to taste)

1. In large pot, bring 12 cups of salted water to boil. Add pasta.

2. After pasta has cooked for 5 minutes, add chickpeas. Continue cooking until pasta is al dente.

3. Meanwhile, heat 2 tablespoons of oil in skillet over medium heat and sauté garlic slivers. Remove from heat once colour begins to change.

4. Drain cooked pasta and chickpeas (reserving all liquid). Add to skillet and return to stovetop over medium heat.

5. Cook for approx. 2 minutes. Mix well.

6. Serve pasta from saucepan; or if you prefer, place ingredients back into reserved liquid for a soup-style meal.

Season with salt and pepper and serve immediately as either a pasta dish or soup.

If you want to thicken the soup, blend some of the chickpeas and return them to the pot. Mix well.

Sogliole Abruzzese
(Oven-Baked Sole)

Lucia (Duronio) Cutrone, Prata D'ansidonia in l'Aquila

(Yield: 4 servings)

8 pieces fresh Sole
1½ cups white wine
1¼ cups Italian breadcrumbs
canola oil (enough for frying fish)
½ cup extra-virgin olive oil
½ tablespoon minced garlic

3 cups diced zucchini
3 cups diced tomatoes
¼ teaspoon finely chopped rosemary
¼ teaspoon finely chopped oregano
salt and freshly ground pepper
1 lemon

1. Rinse sole fillets with water. Pat dry. Dip in wine and dredge in breadcrumbs. Set aside.

2. Warm canola oil in skillet over medium heat and fry sole, approx. 3 minutes on each side. Place on paper towels and set aside.

3. Warm olive oil in another skillet over medium heat and cook garlic until fragrant (approx. 15 seconds). Add zucchini, tomatoes, rosemary, oregano, salt and pepper (to taste). Bring to simmer and cook for approx. 15 minutes.

4. Lightly grease 9x12 casserole dish. Lay cooked sole fillets into casserole dish and cover with zucchini and tomato mixture. Sprinkle with remaining breadcrumbs, squeeze juice of lemon over mixture and cover dish with aluminum foil.

5. Bake in preheated oven at 350°F for 30 minutes.

Serve topped with some of the mixture in the dish, along with lemon wedges.

Pancotto
(Bread Soup with Vegetables)

Daniele Di Padova, Windsor, Ontario

This dish from Abruzzi is called the poor man's dish because nothing went to waste when there was so little.

(Yield: 4 servings)

16 slices Italian bread (½-inch thick)
8 cups broccoli, rapini or potatoes
extra-virgin olive oil
salt and freshly ground pepper
water

1. Slice bread into ½-inch cubes and set aside.

2. Bring 8 cups of salted water to boil and cook broccoli, rapini or potatoes until tender.

3. In 4 individual bowls, add bread cubes and pour in evenly liquid and vegetables. Drizzle each bowl with olive oil and season with salt and pepper.

Serve hot.

It is hearty and can be beefed up with a few additional herbs, but we decided to make it in the original way.

MOLISE

CAPITAL
Campobasso

RED WINE
Biferno

WHITE WINE
Biferno (trebbiano-malvasia)

Sagne e Fagioli
(Pasta Strips and Beans)

Amelia (Tortola) Fasano, Miranda, Isernia

I remember my grandmother cooking this recipe as a young boy, using a terracotta pot next to the fireplace. —Remo

(Yield: 4 servings)

1 pound fresh green beans
(soaked overnight in a large pot of salted water)
1 celery stalk (rough chop)
4 cups flour
1 cup water
2 tablespoons extra-virgin olive oil
2 garlic cloves (minced)
salt and freshly ground pepper

1. Add celery to pot with beans in their soaking water. Bring to boil. Reduce to simmer, and cook for approx. 3 hours.

2. Meanwhile, mound flour on clean working surface and make small well in centre.

3. Add half the water and bring flour in from sides a little at a time, slowly incorporating until well mixed. Continue adding water as needed until slightly elastic but not sticky.

4. Knead dough a few times until formed into a ball. Seal in plastic wrap and allow to sit for 3 hours.

5. Flatten ball into ¾-inch disc.

6. Flour both sides of dough disc and roll out to approx. ⅛-inch thick.

7. Cut dough first into ¼-inch strips, and then into 2 inch lengths. Set aside.

8. Making sure there is plenty of liquid in pot, add noodles to boiling water with beans and celery and cook until al dente. Drain in colander and return to pot.

9. While noodles are cooking, heat olive oil in skillet over medium heat. Add garlic and cook until lightly golden. Add to pot. Stir.

Season with salt and pepper and serve hot.

Pasta Ceci e Cozze
(Pasta with Chickpeas and Mussels)

Maria (Travaglini) Ciucci, Termoli, Campobasso

(Yield: 4 servings)

2 cups water
1 pound fresh mussels (cleaned)
2 tablespoons extra-virgin olive oil
1 garlic clove or more (minced)
1 fresh small chili
14 ounces stewing tomatoes

1 cup dry chickpeas (14 ounce can drained)
½ fish bouillon cube
1 pound quadrotti pasta
(or favourite)
1 rosemary sprig
salt and freshly ground pepper

1. Boil 2 cups salted water in large saucepan over medium heat. Add mussels and a pinch of salt and pepper. Cook covered for approx. 5 minutes. Remove from heat, set aside, and discard any mussels that have not opened.

2. Warm oil in large skillet over medium heat; add garlic, chili, tomatoes, chickpeas, mussels with remaining liquid and bouillon cube. Cook for 15 minutes.

3. Meanwhile, in large pot of boiling salted water cook pasta for half suggested time.

4. Drain pasta (reserving two cups of liquid) and add to skillet with mussels. Add sprig of rosemary, and cook covered for another 5 minutes.

5. Add enough reserved liquid (either from pasta or cooked chickpeas) to ensure sauce does not become too thick.

Season with salt and pepper. Serve immediately.

If using dry chickpeas, the day before place chickpeas and ½ tsp of baking soda in a pot and cover with water approx. 2 inches higher than chickpeas. Allow them to soak 12 to 24 hours. The following day, cook chickpeas in the same pot for approx. 2 hours, drain (but reserve water) and set aside.

This recipe is usually made with quadrotti pasta (flat, ¾-inch squares).

Lessata del Primo Maggio
(Mixed Vegetables)

Antonietta (Romano) Ciarlariello, Limosano, Campobasso

(Yield: 4 servings)

12 ounces each of the following:

roma beans

lentils

corn

chickling beans

dried peas

chickpeas

wheat

spelt (barley)

3 tablespoons extra-virgin olive oil

salt and freshly ground pepper

1. In pot of salted boiling water, cook all vegetables, wheat and barley until tender (approx. 10 minutes).

2. Drain and cool in colander, allowing most of water to seep from vegetables (approx. 15 minutes).

3. Transfer vegetables to large bowl, add olive oil, season with salt and pepper to taste. Toss gently, ensuring everything is coated.

4. Using 2- to 3-inch round ring-molds, fill molds with mixture and press gently to shape. Serve.

   This recipe can be made with an assortment of fresh or canned vegetables. When using canned vegetables, drain, rinse thoroughly and mix. The instructions above are for fresh vegetables that require the cooking process. This may be served warm or at room temperature.

Polpette "Cacio e Uova"
(Meatballs without the Meat)

Carolina (Franceschelli) Marzano, Miranda, Isernia

(Yield: 12+, 4 servings)

4 eggs
1 cup grated Parmigiano-Reggiano
4 slices day-old bread
(crust removed, chopped coarsely)
2 garlic cloves (minced)

1 tablespoon finely chopped parsley
salt and freshly ground pepper
extra-virgin olive or canola* oil
4 cups tomato sauce (see page 308)

1. In large bowl combine eggs, cheese, bread, garlic, parsley and a pinch each salt and pepper (to taste). Mixture should be soft but not dough-like.

2. Scoop out golf-ball-sized portion and roll into ball. Repeat.

3. Heat saucepan with ½ inch of oil over medium heat.

4. Using spider, lower balls into heated oil until saucepan is full.

5. Fry until golden, turning often on all sides. Place on dish lined with paper towel. Allow to sit.

6. In another saucepan, warm your favourite tomato sauce, add polpettes, and cook 15 minutes.

This can be served alone or alongside your favourite pasta.

La Panonta
(4-Layer Sandwich)

Mariuccia (Fasano) Tortola, Miranda, Isernia

This is the ultimate soccer sandwich when watching the game.

(Yield: 8 servings)

extra-virgin olive oil

4 red large sweet peppers
(cored and cut into ½-inch strips)

10 eggs

2 tablespoons Parmesan cheese

salt and freshly ground pepper

15 favourite Italian sausage links
(4-6 inches each)

12-inch round day-old bread
(approx. 3-4 inches thick)

1. Warm ⅛-inch olive oil over medium heat in 8- to 10-inch skillet. Add peppers and a pinch of salt, cooking until almost wilted (15 minutes).

2. Once cooked, place peppers and oil in bowl and set aside.

3. In another bowl, mix eggs, cheese, salt and pepper. Using the previous skillet make a frittata (see page 239) and set aside.

4. Using same skillet again, coat bottom with olive oil over medium heat. Add sausages. Cook for approx. 10 minutes or until browned. Turn sausages and cook for another 10 minutes.

5. Turn off heat and set aside with sausages still in skillet.

6. Cut bread into 5 equal round ¾-inch slices.

ASSEMBLING THE PANONTA:

7. Starting with bottom slice (placed on large cutting board), layer with approx. ¾ of peppers and some juices.

8. Cover with another circle of bread and layer this with the frittata.

9. Add another layer of bread and turn sausages, starting in centre and making circles. Add all juices from pan.

10. Add another layer of bread and cover with remaining peppers and juices.

11. Add final layer of bread and cover with cloth allowing to rest at room temperature for 2 to 3 hours. (Juices should permeate layers.)

When ready to serve, cut in wedges as you would a pizza.

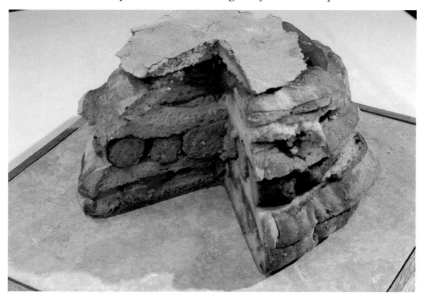

Fiadone con la Verdura
(Rolls Stuffed with Swiss Chard and Anchovies)

Assunta (Maitino) Tortola, Miranda, Isernia

(Yield: 4 servings)

**1 large head Swiss chard
(chopped rough with stems)
2 tablespoons extra-virgin olive oil
2 garlic cloves (minced)**

**12 anchovy fillets (fresh or canned)
(more if you like)
1 basic pizza dough (page 17)
1 egg**

1. Bring large pot of salted water to boil and add chard. Cook 5 to 7 minutes; drain and set aside.

2. Warm oil in skillet over medium heat. Sauté the garlic until fragrant (30 seconds).

3. Add chard and cook for 10 to 15 minutes.

4. Add anchovies and cook approx. 5 minutes. Remove from heat and set aside.

5. Separate pizza dough into 4 balls.

6. On parchment paper roll each ball to ¼-inch thickness.

7. Fill half of rolled dough with Swiss chard mixture.

8. Fold dough over mixture, creating a half-moon shape. Seal all around. Complete other three in same manner.

9. With fork or small knife make approx. 6 slits on each roll.

10. In bowl, beat egg and brush each roll.

11. Line baking sheet with parchment paper and bake rolls in oven preheated to 400°F for 20 to 25 minutes (until golden).

Serve warm or at room temperature.

These can be eaten alone or with your favourite hot tomato sauce as a dip.

Patate Arracanate
(Potatoes with Oregano)

Annunziata (Di Sabato) Federico, Matrice, Campobasso

(Yield: 6 servings)

2 cups day-old Italian bread
(chopped rough without the crust,
not breadcrumbs)
3 tablespoons finely chopped fresh oregano
1 tablespoon finely chopped fresh parsley

1 garlic clove or more (minced)
4 tablespoons extra-virgin olive oil
2 pounds potatoes
(cut in ¾-inch wedges or cubes)
½ cup water

1. In large bowl, add bread, oregano, parsley and garlic. Mix well and set aside.

2. Coat 9x13 casserole dish with tablespoon olive oil and add layer of potatoes.

3. Sprinkle salt on potatoes and add layer of bread mixture.

4. Repeat with more layers as above until all potatoes and mixture have been used.

5. Pour in water around potatoes and drizzle remaining olive oil on top.

6. Cover with lid or tightly seal with aluminum foil.

7. Bake in oven preheated to 350°F for approx. 1 hour.

Serve hot, warm or at room temperature.

Pancetta e Fave
(Fava Beans with Pancetta)

Antonietta (Grassi) Carriero, Gildone, Campobasso

(Yield: 4 servings)

3 tablespoons extra-virgin olive oil

3 garlic cloves (minced)

1 medium onion (diced)

¼ pound pancetta (diced into ¼-inch cubes)

14 ounces fava beans
(if canned, drained and rinsed)

salt and freshly ground pepper (to taste)

1. Warm oil in skillet over medium heat and cook garlic with onions until onions are translucent.

2. Add pancetta and cook for another 10 minutes.

3. Reduce to low heat. Add fava beans and cook for another 5 minutes. Stir occasionally.

Season with salt and pepper. Serve warm.

If using fresh fava beans, cook them first in boiling water for approx. 10 minutes or until tender and drain thoroughly.

Soffritto di Maiale
(Fried Pork and Peppers)

Maria (Mandato) Grassi, Gildone, Campobasso

(Yield: 4 servings)

2 tablespoons extra-virgin olive oil

3 garlic cloves (minced)

1 onion (diced)

1 pound pork shoulder
(cut into bite-size pieces)

salt and freshly ground pepper

1 cup white wine

14 ounces hot pickled peppers
(drained and roughly chopped)

1. Warm oil in large skillet over medium heat. Add garlic with onions and cook until translucent.
2. Add pork and a pinch of salt and pepper. Brown pork on all sides (approx. 10 minutes).
3. Add wine and continue cooking until alcohol has evaporated (3 to 5 minutes).
4. Add peppers, stirring occasionally. Continue cooking until all liquid has evaporated.

Serve immediately.

Cavati al Sugo
(Cavati Pasta with Pork Sauce)

Giovina (Franceschelli) Saccomanna, Isernia

Before I married my husband, my mother would spend every Sunday cooking meals in an attempt to bring my future husband more firmly into the family. This was one of his favourite recipes and is proof that the way to a man's heart is through his stomach. —Maria Pia

CAVATI:
4 cups flour
1 egg
1 cup water
¾ tablespoon salt
SAUCE:
½ cup extra-virgin olive oil
1 onion (diced)
2 pounds lean stewing pork (cut into pieces)
28 ounces crushed tomatoes
1 cup hot water
salt

Cavati:

1. On clean work surface, mound flour and make well in centre.

2. Add egg, water and salt and slowly incorporate flour until well mixed.

3. Knead dough for 10 minutes, until soft. If dough is too sticky add one tablespoon flour at a time; if dough falls apart, add one tablespoon water.

4. Flatten into ¾-inch disc, then roll to ¼-inch thickness.

5. Cut dough into 1½-inch wide strips and then into pieces approx. 1-inch long.

6. Using two fingers centred in noodle, press down and pull noodle towards you, making a full indent on noodle.

7. Set aside on lightly floured surface until you have made all the Cavati.

8. Bring large pot of salted water to boil and add Cavati. Cook until risen to surface.

9. Remove using spider and serve topped with pork sauce.

Sauce:

1. Warm olive oil in saucepan over medium heat and cook onions until slightly browned.

2. Add pork and cook until browned on all sides.

3. Add tomatoes and water and raise to boil. Simmer for 2 hours.

Season with salt to taste.

You can make sauce the day before and reheat it when ready to use.

Brodo di Cardone
(Cardoon or Artichoke Soup)

Maria (Travaglini) Ciucci, Termoli, Campobasso

This recipe is normally made for special occasions (weddings, Christmas, etc).

(Yield: 6 servings)

6 pounds turkey or chicken
(cleaned and innards removed)
2 tablespoons salt (plus more for taste)
2 celery stalks (leaves attached, cut in half)
2 bay leaves
1 nutmeg (left whole)
1 cinnamon stick (approx. 2 inches long)
3 Roma tomatoes (left whole)

1 carrot (peeled and cut in half)
1 onion (cut in half)
3 cardoon leaf stalks
(or 5- to 6-inch artichoke stems, peeled)
zest from 1 lemon
3 tablespoons Parmigiano-Reggiano cheese
2 eggs (beaten)

1. In large pot, add turkey, salt, celery, bay leaves, nutmeg, cinnamon stick, tomatoes, carrot, onion and enough water to cover by 1 or 2 inches.

2. Cook over medium heat till boiling and then reduce to simmer for 2½ to 3 hours. Add boiled water to keep level constant.

3. Remove turkey and set aside. Remove and discard vegetables.

4. Strain broth and return it to clean pot.

5. Break up turkey into small pieces, add to strained broth, and reserve. Keep covered.

6. Meanwhile in another pot of boiling water add cardoons or artichoke stems and cook 6 to 7 minutes, until slightly tender. Drain, cut into ½-inch cubes, and add to pot with turkey.

7. Return turkey and broth to boil, then reduce to simmer and cook for another 5 minutes. Remove from heat.

8. Add lemon zest, cheese and eggs. Give quick stir and allow to sit covered for 2 minutes so eggs will set.

Serve while hot.

Polpette Ripiene con L'Uovo
(Hard-boiled Egg Meatballs in Tomato Sauce)

Assunta (Cirino) Iatonna, Matrice, Campobasso

Whenever my mother-in-law makes a batch of her sauce, she always makes these meatballs with eggs. She normally serves them whole, but I like them sliced and fanned over my pasta. Both my sons consider these meatballs a special treat, since they only have them at Nonna's house. I personally like them as a meatball sandwich on crusty Italian bread. —Giuliano

(Yield: 6 meatballs, tennis ball-sized)

MEATBALL INGREDIENTS:

1½ pounds ground veal

1½ pounds ground beef

3 small eggs

6 tablespoons grated Romano cheese

6 tablespoons breadcrumbs

1 teaspoon paprika

¼ cup finely chopped parsley

1 teaspoon salt

6 small hard-boiled eggs (shelled and cooled)

1. In large bowl, thoroughly mix all meat, then add eggs and re-mix.

2. Add cheese, breadcrumbs, paprika, and parsley. Salt and mix again. It should be slightly sticky. If not, add more breadcrumbs and set aside.

SAUCE INGREDIENTS:

1 zucchini (diced)

1 large carrot (diced)

1 celery stalk (diced)

1 green pepper (diced)

½ cup vegetable oil

6 cans whole peeled San Marzano tomatoes (28 ounces each)

3. In food processor add all sauce ingredients and purée (usually in batches). Set aside.

4. Warm oil in large saucepan over medium heat and add 1/3 meat mixture, stirring often until lightly browned.

5. Add sauce purée. Bring to boil, reduce heat, and simmer partially covered for 2 hours. Stir occasionally. Season with salt and more Romano cheese to taste.

6. When sauce has started simmering, prepare meatballs. Take one hard-boiled egg at a time and pack tight, surrounding with ¼ inch of meat mixture.

7. Add egg meatballs (raw) into sauce; they will cook over the 2 + hours.

8. If there is any meat left over, put it in the sauce.

If you have jarred peeled tomatoes or your own homemade sauce, use that instead.

PUGLIA

CAPITAL
Bari

RED WINE
Primitivo di Manduria

WHITE WINE
Salice Salentino

Orecchiette con Cime di Rapa
(Orecchiette with Broccoli Raab)

Anthony Cutrone, Palo del Colle, Bari

Orecchiette is an ear-shaped pasta prevalent in southern Italy, especially Apulia, and is often paired with greens or vegetables such as broccoli, rapini, and cauliflower; feast-day orecchiette calls for robust meat sauces instead.

(Yield: 4 servings)

2 tablespoons salt
2 tablespoons extra-virgin olive oil
4 garlic cloves (minced)
2 salted anchovies
(deboned, gutted, rinsed, and chopped),
or 4 anchovy fillets packed in olive oil
(drained and chopped. Optional but delicious.)

2 dried chili peppers
(crumbled or ½ teaspoon chili flakes)
2 bunches (1 pound) rapini (chopped with yellow buds and tough stems removed)
1 pound orecchiette
1 cup freshly grated Pecorino Romano
(omit if using anchovies)

1. Bring large pot of salted water to boil.

2. Warm olive oil in small skillet over medium-low heat. Add garlic and cook 30 seconds until fragrant.

3. Stir in anchovies and crush into olive oil with back of a fork.

4. Add chilies and keep warm on lowest possible heat.

5. Add rapini and orecchiette to boiling water. Cook until orecchiette is al dente, stirring often.

6. Drain and return to pot, pour in warm garlic/anchovy oil sauce from skillet. Mix well.

Top with the Pecorino Romano if you like, and serve immediately.

Pittule
(Fried Caper Fritters)

Meli Fernanda, Parabita, Lecce

Pittule are balls of dough fried in very hot oil and typical to the region of Puglia. Although the standard is basic fried dough, this recipe calls for the addition of capers and tomatoes; you can substitute cauliflower or anchovies, or turn it into a sweet if so desired.

(Yield: approx. 24)

1 cup warm water
1½ teaspoons instant yeast
5 cups all-purpose flour
1 teaspoon salt

3 tablespoons extra-virgin olive oil
canola oil, for frying and for coating the dough
1 tablespoon capers
1 cup diced tomatoes

1. Add yeast to bowl with warm water. Wait 10 minutes for yeast to dissolve.

2. In another bowl add flour, salt, olive oil and mix. Slowly add water and yeast mixture, mixing until dough ball is soft and sticky.

3. Coat sides of large bowl with oil and place ball in it. Cover with plastic wrap and place in warm draft-proof place. Allow to rise for 2 hours.

4. When the ball has doubled in size, remove from bowl and knead flat. Incorporate tomatoes and capers slowly into dough. Form into rounds the size of golf balls.

5. Heat saucepan with approx. 3 inches oil. When oil starts boiling, drop pittule into oil with tablespoon, frying until golden brown. Remove with spider.

Sprinkle with salt and serve warm!

Although we used all-purpose flour, chickpea flour is commonly found in many pitulle recipes.

Agnello al Forno con Patate
(Roasted Lamb with Potatoes)

Alessio Grilli, Monte Sant'Angelo, Foggia

(Yield: 4 servings)

4 lamb chops (¼ pound each)
1 rosemary sprig (leaves only)
4 garlic cloves (minced)
¼ cup grated Parmesan cheese
¼ cup breadcrumbs

2 tablespoons finely chopped parsley
salt and freshly ground pepper
2 teaspoons extra-virgin olive oil
5 potatoes
1 cup water (optional white wine)

1. In bowl add rosemary, garlic, cheese, breadcrumbs, parsley, salt, pepper and olive oil. Mix thoroughly.

2. Scrub potatoes (leave skin on) and cut into large wedges.

3. Add potatoes to seasoning mixture and toss until well-coated.

4. Put chops in oven pan, pour in water (or wine), and add seasoned potatoes, making sure to use all seasoning in bowl.

5. Seal pan with aluminum foil and roast in oven preheated to 350°F for 1½ hours.

6. For last 30 minutes, remove aluminum foil, allowing potatoes to become crisp.

7. Plate lamb chops with potatoes and drizzle with juice from pan.

Serve warm.

Minestrone Pugliese
(Minestrone with Rapini)

Vanda (Otello) Dilillo, Brindisi

(Yield: 4 servings)

2 pounds rapini
(stems removed and roughly chopped)
1 onion (diced)
5 tablespoons extra-virgin olive oil
1 pinch red chili powder

1 pinch black pepper
¼ pound tubetti (little rigatoni)
salt
grated Romano cheese

1. Bring large pot of salted water to boil, add chopped rapini stems, and cook approx. 10 minutes. Drain, reserving water.

2. In food processor, add cooked rapini stems, onions and process for approx. 30 seconds until slightly pasty.

3. Warm 3 tablespoons oil in large saucepan over medium heat. Add processed rapini, chili powder and pepper, and cook approx. 5 minutes.

4. Add 7 cups of reserved liquid and cook for an hour.

5. Add tubetti, rapini leaves, and salt to taste. Cook until tubetti is al dente. Remove from heat, sprinkle a handful of cheese and drizzle with remaining olive oil.

Serve hot.

Braciole al Sugo
(Stuffed Beef Rolls with Tomato Sauce)

Lucia (Notarangelo) Grilli, Monte Sant'Angelo, Foggia

(Yield: 4 servings)

4 thin beef slices
4 thin pancetta slices
CHEESE FILLING:
1 cup grated Romano cheese
¼ cup fresh parsley (finely chopped)
1 red chili (finely chopped)
2 garlic cloves (minced)

2 tablespoons extra-virgin olive oil
½ cup onion (diced)
½ cup red or white wine
4 cups tomato sauce
¼ cup fresh basil (finely chopped)
salt and freshly ground black pepper

1. In bowl mix cheese, parsley, chili and garlic thoroughly and set aside.

2. Beef slices should be thin. If not, lay beef slices on sheet of plastic wrap, cover with another sheet, and use the flat side of a kitchen mallet to lightly pound beef until ¼-inch thick.

3. Place pancetta slice on top of beef and spread ¼ of cheese filling on top. Roll the braciole tightly and secure with toothpick. Season with salt and pepper.

4. Warm oil in skillet over medium heat. Add onions, and cook until translucent.

5. Add braciole to skillet and cook for approx. 1 minute per side, then add wine and allow alcohol to evaporate (approx. 3 minutes).

6. Add tomato sauce and basil, reduce heat to low and cook for another 7 to 10 minutes. Season to taste.

7. Transfer braciole to serving plate, increase heat to medium, and cook till liquid is reduced by half. Pour liquid onto plated braciole.

Serve immediately.

Patate e Baccalà al Forno
(Oven-baked Cod and Potatoes)

Lucia (Grilli) Otello, Foggia

(Yield: 4 servings)

1½ pounds baccalà (cod fillets)
5 teaspoons extra-virgin olive oil (plus extra)
1 cup water (optional white wine)
1 cup breadcrumbs

1 garlic clove (minced)
1 teaspoon freshly ground black pepper
¼ cup parsley (chopped fine)
6 potatoes (cleaned, cut into wedges, skin on)

1. Lightly grease bottom of oven pan with 2 teaspoons of oil, layer in cod fillets, and pour in water (or wine).

2. In bowl combine breadcrumbs, garlic, pepper, parsley and remaining oil. Mix well. Add cut potatoes and toss.

3. Add potatoes to pan and drizzle lightly with more oil.

4. Seal pan with aluminum foil and bake in oven preheated to 350°F for 1½ hours, removing foil for last 30 minutes.

Serve plated with pan juices.

Traditionally this recipe is made using dry salted cod, giving it a slightly different flavour. Refer to page 306 for preparation of salted cod.

Spaghetti con Seppie e Piselli
(Spaghetti, Cuttlefish and Peas)

Rosa (Calamita) Silvestri, Bari

(Yield: 4 servings)

1 pound spaghetti
1 pound cuttlefish (cut into strips)
2 teaspoons extra-virgin olive oil
2 garlic cloves (minced)
1 onion (diced)

½ cup white wine
16 ounces crushed tomatoes
1 cup peas (fresh or frozen)
2 teaspoons finely chopped parsley
salt and freshly ground pepper

1. Warm oil in large skillet over low heat and sauté garlic and onions until onions are translucent.

2. Add strips of cuttlefish. Stir well and continue cooking for 5 minutes. Add wine, cook for 5 minutes, and then add tomatoes. Salt and pepper to taste. Increase heat to medium and once boiling, reduce to low and allow sauce to simmer partially covered for approx. 30 minutes.

3. Add peas in last 10 minutes. Sprinkle half the parsley in last 5 minutes. Stir well.

4. While sauce is cooking, bring pot of salted water to boil, add spaghetti and cook until al dente.

5. Drain, add spaghetti to sauce, mix thoroughly, and cook for another minute. Remove from heat and sprinkle remaining parsley.

Serve immediately.

Zuppa di Cozze alla Tarantina
(Mussel Soup)

Leonarda (Notarangelo) Guerra, Manfredonia, Foggia

(Yield: 4 servings)

2 pounds mussels (scrubbed and cleaned)

2 tablespoons extra-virgin olive oil

2 garlic cloves (smashed)

½ teaspoon chili flakes

12 ounces tomato sauce

1 teaspoon salt

2 tablespoons finely chopped parsley

toasted bread

1. Warm oil in deep saucepan over medium heat. Add garlic and sauté until garlic is golden, then remove and discard garlic.

2. Add chili flakes, tomato sauce, and salt; reduce heat to low and cook for approx. 10 minutes.

3. Add cleaned mussels and parsley. Stir well. Cook covered until the mussels have opened (10 minutes). Discard any that have not opened.

Serve immediately with the juices and toasted bread.

If using fresh mussels, rinse under cold running water, making sure to remove beards. Discard any mussels that do not close when cleaning or open after they have been cooked.

Orecchiette di Primavera–pasta Fredda
(Orecchiette with Vegetables)

Rosa (Calamita) Silvestri, Bari

(Yield: 4 servings)

1 pound orecchiette
extra-virgin olive oil
1 pound asparagus
(cleaned, trimmed, 1½-inch pieces)
2 cups peas (fresh or frozen)
3 tomatoes (chopped)

4 green onions, white and green parts (chopped)
1 red bell pepper (chopped)
salt and freshly ground pepper
½ cup shaved Pecorino or Parmesan cheese
2 tablespoons finely chopped parsley

1. In large pot of salted boiling water, cook orecchiette until al dente, drain and return it to large bowl; sprinkle with olive oil to prevent sticking, mix well and allow to cool completely.

2. In small saucepan of boiling water, cook asparagus until fork-tender. Remove and allow to cool.

3. In the same pot of boiling water, blanch peas, drain, and allow to cool.

4. Add all vegetables to pasta bowl and season with salt and pepper, tossing with extra oil if required.

5. Garnish with cheese and parsley.

Serve at room temperature.

This dish can be made the day before, refrigerated and served cold. When ready to serve, a touch of good quality balsamic vinegar is optional but excellent. To preserve freshness after cooking, run pasta, asparagus and peas under cold water.

Cozze Piene alla Barese
(Stuffed Mussels with Tomato Sauce)

Elena (Cataneo) Otello, Bari

(Yield: 4 servings)

1 pound day-old bread

FILLING:

2 eggs

2 garlic cloves (minced)

1 thin slice Mortadella (finely diced)

1 teaspoon freshly grated nutmeg

¼ cup finely chopped parsley

1 teaspoon salt

1 teaspoon freshly ground pepper

1 cup grated Parmigiano cheese

2 pounds cleaned mussels

4 tablespoons olive oil

2 garlic cloves

5 cups tomato sauce

1. Soak bread in bowl of water until soft. Remove and squeeze out as much water as possible.

2. In large bowl add bread, eggs, half of garlic, mortadella, nutmeg, parsley, salt, pepper, cheese and mix thoroughly. Set aside.

3. Heat large pot filled with ¼ inch of water. Add mussels and cook covered for approx. 10 minutes, or until all mussels have opened. ***Discard any mussels that have not opened.***

4. Fill each mussel with bread mixture and close using butcher string.

5. Warm oil in large skillet over medium heat. Add remaining garlic, tomato sauce and cook for approx. 10 minutes.

6. Add tied mussels and cook for an additional 20 minutes.

Serve warm, with toasted Italian bread.

CAMPANIA

CAPITAL
Napoli

RED WINE
Rosso Cilento

WHITE WINE
Greco di Tufo

Valle D'Aosta

Piemonte

Liguria

Lombardia

Trentino-Alto Adige

Friuli-Venezia Giulia

Veneto

Emilia-Romagna

Toscana

Umbria

Marche

Lazio

Abruzzo

Molise

Campania

Puglia

Basilicata

Calabria

Sardegna

Sicilia

Ligurian Sea

Adriatic Sea

Tyrrhenian Sea

Mediterranean Sea

Ionian Sea

Melanzane al Funghetto
(Eggplant Salad)

Assunta (Testa) Sorrentino, Napoli

(Yield: 4 servings)

¼ cup extra-virgin olive oil

2 eggplants (remove centre with seeds and cube)

1 garlic clove (minced)

28 ounces tomatoes (cubed)

1 teaspoon salt

3 basil leaves (chopped rough)

1. Warm oil in skillet over medium heat. Add cubed eggplant and cook until lightly brown. Using slotted spoon, remove eggplant from pan and set aside.

2. In same skillet, add garlic and cook until fragrant (30 seconds). Add tomatoes, salt, basil and simmer for approx. 15 minutes.

3. Add eggplant to sauce and continue cooking for 15 minutes.

Serve warm.

Pasta e Piselli
(Pasta and Peas)

Angela Testa, Napoli

This type of dish is a lifesaver because it is quick and easy to make, especially when you do not feel like cooking. Although easy to make, it is very satisfying.

(Yield: 4 servings)

8 cups water	¼ cup parsley chopped
14 ounces peas (fresh or canned)	1 onion (diced)
1 tablespoon extra-virgin olive oil	1 pound tubetti (or favourite short pasta)
1 teaspoon salt	Parmesan cheese

1. In large saucepan over medium heat, add all ingredients except for tubetti and cheese, and allow to boil for 2 minutes.

2. Reduce heat to low and continue cooking for 45 minutes.

3. When you are ready to add tubetti, increase to medium heat. Once mixture has returned to boil add tubetti (or your favourite short pasta) and cook until al dente.

Serve immediately with a sprinkle of cheese.

Peperoni con Olive e Capperi
(Roasted Peppers with Olives and Capers)

Assunta (Testa) Sorrentino, Napoli

(Yield: 4 servings)

4 red peppers
4 tablespoons extra-virgin olive oil
2 tablespoons breadcrumbs
1 garlic clove (minced)

10 black olives (pitted and chopped)
1 tablespoon capers
salt and freshly ground pepper

1. Preheat oven to 400°F.

2. Place peppers on baking sheet and coat with 2 tablespoons olive oil. Roast in oven until skin is blackened and blistered (approx. 15 minutes). Place in bowl, covered with plastic wrap and allow to cool.

3. Remove and discard skin, de-seed and cut peppers into strips.

4. Warm remaining oil in skillet over low heat. Add peppers, breadcrumbs, garlic, olives, capers and season with salt and pepper. Cook for approx. 15 minutes.

Serve while warm or at room temperature.

As an alternative to using the oven, the same process can be used with a BBQ, making sure that the heat is set at high.

Lasagna con Polpette
(Lasagna with Meatballs)

Guseppina (Testa) Fiorito, Napoli

(Yield: 4 servings)

1 pound lasagna noodles
5 cups tomato sauce (see page 308)
1 pound Ricotta cheese (broken into pieces)

30 small meatballs (see page 270)
1 pound shredded Mozzarella cheese
2 cups grated Parmigiano-Reggiano cheese

1. In pot of salted boiling water, add lasagna noodles and cook for approx. 5 minutes. Drain and run under cold water to stop cooking process. Put in bowl with a little olive oil so noodles do not stick together. Set aside.

2. Using 9x13 oven pan spread layer of sauce evenly, covering entire bottom of pan.

3. Add layer of lasagna noodles, Ricotta cheese, meatballs, Mozzarella cheese, sprinkle Parmigiano cheese and another ladle of sauce.

4. Continue layering until pan is filled. Finish top layer with cheeses and tomato sauce and a last sprinkle of Parmigiano- Reggiano.

5. Cook in oven preheated to 350°F for approx. 1 hour.

6. Remove and allow to sit for 5 minutes.

Serve immediately.

One option to meatballs is to use about 1 pound pre-browned ground beef. If you prefer to make a vegetarian lasagna, use shredded zucchini or your choice of another vegetable in its place.

Frittata di Spaghetti
(Spaghetti Frittata)

Daniela (Sorrentino) Pastorius, Napoli

As explained on page 239, frittatas are very versatile when it comes to adding things to them. Here is the perfect solution for that leftover pasta. It is delicious and easy to make.

(Yield: 4 servings)

2 tablespoons extra-virgin olive oil

4 eggs

¼ cup Parmesan cheese

½ teaspoon salt and freshly ground pepper

leftover pasta (¼ pound pre-cooked)

1. Whisk eggs in bowl, add cheese, pasta and season with salt and pepper.
2. Warm oil in skillet over low heat, spread pasta mixture evenly in skillet and cook until bottom is set.
3. Place skillet in oven preheated to 350°F and bake until top is golden brown.

Serve hot or cold.

Insalata di Cavolfiore
(Cauliflower Salad)

Angela Testa, Napoli

(Yield: 4 servings)

1 cauliflower head (cut into florets)

2 cups black and green olives (pitted)

2 garlic cloves (diced)

½ cup pickled peppers (mild or hot, chopped)

¼ cup fresh parsley (chopped fine)

2 tablespoons white vinegar

¼ cup extra-virgin olive oil

salt and freshly ground pepper

1. Using pot with steamer basket, steam florets for 10 minutes or until tender (but still firm).

2. Remove and add florets, olives, garlic, peppers, parsley, vinegar and oil. Season with salt and pepper in large bowl and toss well.

Serve warm or at room temperature.

In place of the vinegar, you can substitute lemon juice. To give it a little kick, chopped anchovies go well.

Pane e Pomodoro
(Crusted Bread with Tomatoes)

Lina Sorrentino, Napoli

A simple alternative option to Bruschetta.

(Yield: 12+ servings)

1 day-old Italian bread loaf
2 tablespoons extra-virgin olive oil
3 tomatoes (sliced ¼-inch thick)

3 garlic cloves (sliced thin)
6 large fresh basil leaves (chiffonade)
salt and freshly ground pepper

1. Slice bread to 1-inch rounds and brush entire surface with olive oil.

2. Put slices on broil pan and broil at 400°F until golden (approx. 4 minutes), making sure they do not burn.

3. Remove from oven and immediately layer.

4. Add 2 tomato slices, a few garlic slices, some basil and season with salt and pepper and a final drizzle of olive oil.

Serve warm as a great appetizer (optional, sprinkle with Parmesan cheese).

Frittata

Tina (Sorrentino) Tuer, Napoli

Here is what we call the basic frittata. Frittatas and omelettes differ in a few ways. Frittatas always contain an optional ingredient that is normally combined with the beaten mixture while still raw. It is cooked over low heat, more slowly than an omelette until the bottom is set but the top is slightly runny. A frittata is not folded over as is an omelette, but is either turned over or finished off in an oven or under a broiler. Frittatas are normally divided into slices that may be served cold or hot alongside a salad or fresh bread. You can add so many different things while cooking the onions and before adding the eggs; experiment with sausage, prosciutto, asparagus or anything else that you like.

(Yield: 4 servings)

6 eggs
2 tablespoons extra-virgin olive oil

½ cup onions (diced or sliced)
½ teaspoon salt and pepper

1. Warm oil in ovenproof skillet over low heat. Sauté onions until translucent.

2. Meanwhile, whisk eggs with salt and pepper.

3. Add eggs to skillet, making sure they are evenly spread, and cook until bottom is set and golden and top is still slightly runny.

4. Remove skillet from heat and place in oven preheated to 350°F. Bake until set and golden.*

Once set, allow to rest a few minutes, then cut into wedges and serve.

*Or put in oven under broiler for 5 to 7 minutes until set and golden. Make sure to use a pan that is oven/broiler safe.

Salsa Bolognese
(Bolognese Sauce)

Giuseppina (Testa) Fiorito, Napoli

Bolognese sauce is a meat-based sauce for pasta originating from Bologna, Italy. It is customarily used to dress tagliatelle and can be used in many pasta recipes. Here is a regional variation not to be confused with the Bolognese Ragu recipe.

(Yield: 4 servings)

1 tablespoon extra-virgin olive oil	½ pound lean ground beef
½ onion (diced)	5½ ounces tomato paste
1 carrot (diced)	28 ounces crushed tomatoes
1 celery stalk (diced)	salt and freshly ground pepper

1. Warm oil in large saucepan over medium heat. Add onion, carrot and celery and cook until tender (approx. 8 minutes).

2. Add ground beef and cook until it starts to turn a light brown.

3. Stir in tomato paste and add crushed tomatoes. Once boiling, reduce heat to low; season with salt and pepper and let simmer for 1 to 2 hours.

Serve with your favourite pasta.

For a vegetarian version, omit the beef and add triple the quantities of the diced vegetables.

Panzarotti
(Cheese Balls)

Alessandro Sorrentino, Napoli

This is a version of the standard panzarotti but is a ball shape versus a half moon. Instead of using dough for the outside, a potato mixture has taken its place.

(Yield: 8 medium-sized balls)

4 potatoes (peeled and quartered)
¼ cup grated Parmesan cheese
1 egg (yolk and white separated)

1 teaspoon salt
4 ounces Mozzarella
½ cup breadcrumbs
canola oil

1. Bring saucepan of salted water with potatoes to boil and cook until fork-tender.

2. Drain and mash potatoes. Once cooled, add Parmesan, egg yolk and salt. Mix well.

3. Take a small amount of mixture and flatten to 3- to 4-inch square and place a piece of Mozzarella cheese in centre.

4. Gently fold the sides to make a ball shape, pressing lightly to hold together. Continue until all mixture has been used.

5. Prepare 2 bowls, one with beaten egg whites, and one with breadcrumbs.

6. Warm saucepan with 2 inches of canola oil over medium heat.

7. Roll a cheese ball in egg white, and then in breadcrumbs. Using spider insert balls in hot canola oil, frying until golden.

8. Remove with spider onto paper-lined bowl.

Serve warm with a sprinkle of salt.

The flat version can be made like a standard panzarotti in a half moon shape and pan fried instead.

Pasta al Limone
(Lemon Pasta)

La Preferita (Nicola), Amalfi, Salerno

We spent a week in Amalfi and by far the best restaurant we visited was La Preferita. The panoramic view over the Amalfi Bay was wonderful, as was the food and the attention of the owner, Nicola. On our first visit, we started with some prosecco as we chose our dishes – all wonderful. On the second visit we had the simplest pasta – Limone. It was absolutely fantastic and provided us with one of our best memories of the Amalfi region. We even persuaded Nicola to share the recipe with us. —David Hughes and Anna Piazza

(Yield: 4 servings)

1 pound penne, spaghetti or linguine

SAUCE:

½ cup extra-virgin olive oil, plus extra for serving

2 teaspoons grated lemon zest

2 medium-size lemons juiced

½ cup finely grated Parmesan cheese, plus extra for serving

½ teaspoon salt and freshly ground pepper

¼ cup freshly chopped parsley

1. Bring large pot of salted water to boil. Add pasta and cook until al dente.

2. While pasta is cooking grate and juice lemons.

3. In a bowl whisk oil, lemon zest, lemon juice, cheese, salt, pepper and parsley.

4. Drain pasta, reserving 1½ cups of cooking liquid.

5. Return pasta to pot and add oil/lemon mixture. Mix well.

6. Add a little of reserved pasta water as needed to thin out.

Serve immediately, drizzled with extra-virgin olive oil and Parmesan cheese.

Spaghetti con Vitello alla Pizzaiola
(Spaghetti and Veal)

Alessandro Sorrentino, Napoli

(Yield: 4 servings)

1 pound spaghetti	28 ounces diced tomatoes
4 slices veal/beef cutlets	½ cup water (or wine)
1 tablespoon extra-virgin olive oil	½ teaspoon fresh oregano (chopped fine)
1 garlic clove (minced)	1 teaspoon salt

1. Warm oil in skillet over medium heat and cook garlic until fragrant (30 seconds).

2. Add tomatoes, water, oregano and salt and stir. Once boiling, reduce heat to low and allow to simmer covered for 1 hour, stirring occasionally. Add a little water if mixture thickens too much.

3. While sauce is cooking, bring pot of salted water to boil and cook pasta.

4. While pasta is cooking, add cutlets to sauce and cook for 5 to 8 minutes.

5. Drain pasta and serve on individual plates. Add a cutlet and top with sauce.

Serve with a sprinkle of Parmesan cheese (optional).

BASILICATA

CAPITAL
Potenza

RED WINE
Aglianico

WHITE WINE
Grottino di Roccanova (Malvasia Bianca di Basilicata)

Valle D'Aosta

Piemonte

Lombardia

Trentino-Alto Adige

Friuli-Venezia Giulia

Veneto

Liguria

Emilia-Romagna

Ligurian Sea

Toscana

Marche

Umbria

Adriatic Sea

Lazio

Abruzzo

Molise

Campania

Basilicata

Puglia

Sardegna

Tyrrhenian Sea

Calabria

diterranean Sea

Sicilia

Ionian Sea

Ravioli con Ricotta Dolce
(Ravioli Stuffed with Sweet Ricotta)

Maria (Gruosso) Mecca, Bella, Potenza

On most farms around the hills and mountains they raised sheep for milk to make Ricotta cheese. They would also sell lambs in the spring to the local butcher. Nearby farmers would take turns looking after the sheep, and they also took turns to make the cheese, most of which was sold to dairy stores in town. In turn they would purchase staples such as sugar, salt, oil, etc. Only a few times a year would ravioli with sweet Ricotta be made, making this a special treat.

—Tony

(Yield: 4 servings)

1 pound lasagna noodles
1 pound Ricotta
¼ cup finely chopped mint
sugar

1 egg-white (beaten lightly)
chili flakes (optional)
1 sprig mint leaves (for garnish)
Pecorino cheese

1. Prepare pasta dough (pages 306-7) and make 12 long lasagna-style pasta sheets (or more), each 3x12 inches. Cover with a clean towel until ready to use.

2. In large bowl, add Ricotta and chopped mint. Start with half a cup of sugar and mix well by hand (or use a blender). Check for sweetness and continue adding sugar until it is to your taste.

3. On floured surface place strip of pasta and mark into 4 equal squares. In centre of each square add tablespoon of sweet Ricotta mixture.

4. Brush egg-white around whole pasta strip and in between Ricotta fillings.

5. Place another sheet of pasta directly on top,

pressing firmly in middle and along sides, removing any air pockets.

6. Cut the pasta strip giving you twelve 3x3-inch ravioli. Using a fork, press firmly around each ravioli to seal. Place on floured tray and cover with clean towel until ready to use. Do the same for remaining pasta strips.

7. Bring large pot of salted water to boil. Add ravioli and cook. When they rise to surface they are done. Using spider, gently remove and place equally on four plates. Top with scoop of your favourite sauce, freshly grated Pecorino cheese, a sprinkle of chili flakes and garnish with a few mint leaves.

Lasagna con Ricotta Dolce
(Lasagna with Sweet Ricotta)

Maria (Ignico) Gugliotta, Bella, Potenza

This recipe is very similar to the ravioli with sweet Ricotta, because we start off with flat pasta sheets. Back in Italy 50-60 years ago, lasagna was cooked differently; ovens were often not available on farms. The lasagna in this case, as in many other cooking situations, was baked in a casserole with a lid, then placed in a fireplace with hot coals on the bottom and on top. —Tony

(Yield: 6 servings)

1 pound lasagna noodles
extra-virgin olive oil
2 pounds Ricotta cheese

¼ cup finely chopped mint
sugar (to taste)
6 cups tomato sauce
Parmigiano cheese

1. Prepare pasta dough and make lasagna egg noodles as per instructions on pages 306-7 (or use store-bought noodles).

2. Bring pot of salted water to boil and cook lasagna noodles for 3 minutes, until they have softened. Drain and run under cold water to stop cooking process. Once noodles have cooled, add to bowl with a little olive oil, so they will not stick together, and toss gently.

3. In large bowl, add Ricotta and chopped mint. Start with half a cup of sugar and mix. Check for sweetness and continue adding sugar until it is to your liking.

4. Grease 9x13 oven dish and spread layer of tomato sauce over bottom. Add layer of noodles; spread some of Ricotta and ladle of sauce. Continue building layers until all ingredients have been used. Finish with layer of tomato sauce and good sprinkle of Parmigiano cheese.

5. Cover with aluminum foil and cook in oven preheated to 350°F for 1 hour.

Remove foil for last half-hour of cooking and serve hot.

Agnello al Morbido
(Lamb with Sauce)

Connie-Rosa (Ciampa) Gugliotta, Marcedusa, Catanzaro (Calabria)

(Yield: 8 servings)

2 pounds lamb chops
MARINADE:
3 garlic cloves (sliced)
2 rosemary sprigs
1 tablespoon fresh oregano (chopped fine)
¼ cup fresh lemon juice
½ cup white wine
1 teaspoon salt
1 teaspoon freshly ground pepper

4 tablespoons extra-virgin olive oil
2 garlic cloves (sliced)
½ cup white wine
1 rosemary sprig
¼ cup lemon juice
¼ cup grappa (or rye)
28 ounces diced tomatoes
chilies (optional)

1. Add lamb chops and marinade ingredients to ziplock bag. Seal bag and shake everything well and marinate in refrigerator overnight. Shake every few hours.

2. After marinating, remove lamb chops and discard marinade.

3. Warm oil in large skillet over medium heat. Cook garlic until fragrant (30 seconds).

4. Add lamb chops and sear approx. 1 minute per side.

5. Add wine, rosemary, lemon juice, grappa,* tomatoes, chilies, and season with salt and pepper. Mix well and once boiling reduce heat to low.

6. Cook covered for 1 to 1½ hours, stirring occasionally. Make sure there are fluids and, if not, add additional water or wine, as necessary.

Serve with crusty Italian bread.

*Whenever adding any spirits to a pan, make sure pan is away from heat to prevent accidental ignition.

Cavatelli con Peperoni Arrostiti
(Cavatelli with Roasted Peppers)

Maria (Ignico) Gugliotta, Bella, Potenza

(Yield: 4 servings)

1 green pepper	3 garlic cloves (sliced thin)
1 yellow pepper	½ teaspoon chili flakes (a pinch)
1 red pepper	1 tablespoon salt
1 orange pepper	1 teaspoon freshly ground pepper
1 pound cavatelli	¼ cup chopped fresh parsley
4 tablespoons extra-virgin olive oil	

1. On hot grill or BBQ (on high heat), grill peppers whole until charred black on all sides, then place in paper bag until cooled. Remove blackened skin, seeds, membranes, stems and cut into strips. Set aside.

2. Bring large pot of salted water to boil, add cavatelli and cook until al dente.

3. While pasta is cooking, warm oil in large skillet over medium heat. Add sliced garlic and sauté until fragrant (30 seconds). Add peppers, chili flakes, season with salt and pepper and cook for 4 minutes.

4. Drain cavatelli and add to skillet along with half of parsley. Mix well and cook for another minute.

5. Remove from heat, place in large bowl, add remaining parsley, toss again and serve immediately.

This dish is always better with homemade pasta. You can also substitute cavatelli with penne-rigate or farfalle pastas.

Ciambotta
(Warm Vegetable Salad)

Teresa (Martone) Tarantino, Bella, Potenza

This is a tasteful and colourful dish that rural Italians made during the hardships they faced during the Second World War. The vegetables replaced the meat which was either not available or unaffordable. —Tony

(Yield: 4 servings)

¼ cup extra-virgin olive oil

1 large onion (sliced ¼-inch)

1 garlic clove (sliced thin)

2 red peppers (sliced 1-inch strips)

2 green peppers (sliced 1-inch strips)

14 ounces diced tomatoes

1 teaspoon salt

1 teaspoon pepper

1 teaspoon chili flakes

4 basil leaves

2 small zucchini (sliced 2-inch strips)

2 eggs beaten, optional*

1. Warm oil in large skillet over medium-high heat. Add onions and garlic and cook for approx. 1 minute. Add peppers and cook for another 3 minutes. Add diced tomatoes with its juices, add salt and pepper and chili flakes to taste. Mix well. Add basil.

2. Once boiling, reduce heat, and simmer for 15 minutes.

3. Add zucchini strips and continue cooking for another 5 minutes.

4. Remove from heat, discard basil leaves.

   Serve with crusty Italian bread.

   *Optional: when pan is removed from heat pour in beaten eggs immediately, stirring continuously. The residual heat will cook the eggs.

Gallina con Patate al Forno
(Roasted Chicken and Potatoes)

Tony Gugliotta, Bella, Potenza

In Basilicata, meat dishes were rare, because most poultry, lamb, pork, beef and rabbit was sold to butchers from neighbouring towns and cities. The "fiera" was where all of the farmers would meet on the outskirts of town to either buy or sell their stock. It was quite the scene with the local zingari or salesmen bargaining with farmers in search of deals. —Tony

(Yield: 4 servings)

1 whole chicken, approx. 3 pounds
(cut into pieces)
6 potatoes (peeled and cut into wedges)
1 tablespoon salt
1 teaspoon pepper

1 tablespoon paprika
2 rosemary sprigs
¼ teaspoon chili flakes
¼ cup extra-virgin olive oil

1. In large bowl, add potatoes, salt, pepper, paprika, rosemary, chili flakes and oil. Toss until potatoes are well-coated.

2. Spread potatoes in large, lightly greased oven dish.

3. Add chicken to bowl and toss with remaining seasoning. Add to oven dish, spreading evenly.

4. Roast uncovered in oven preheated to 375°F for 20 minutes.

5. Lower oven temperature to 350°F and continue cooking for another hour or until chicken juice runs clear and potatoes are crispy.

Serve immediately.

L'Acquasale
(Eggs, Bread, Onion Breakfast)

Vincenzo Gugliotta, Bella, Potenza

During my childhood, living on a farm with my parents and grandparents, I had to do chores after school. When those responsibilities were laid on a 7 to 8 year old, playing was outlawed and if it was pursed, the wooden spoon came into play. Sometimes, early in the morning my father would send me to the chicken coup to pick up the eggs and put together a simple breakfast. —Tony

(Yield: 4 servings)

6 cups water
4 teaspoons salt
4 eggs

2 tablespoons extra-virgin olive oil
6 green onions (diced, white and green parts)
1 loaf day-old Italian bread

1. In saucepan bring water and salt to boil. Crack and add eggs to water and cook for 3 minutes.

2. Meanwhile, warm oil in skillet over medium heat. Sauté onions for approx. 5 minutes and add to pot with eggs. Gently mix, cooking for another 3 minutes.

3. Add pieces of day-old bread filling to 4 bowls.

4. Add egg to each bowl on top of bread and pour in enough water/onion mixture to moisten bread without turning it into mush.

On those cold winter mornings, this will not only satisfy you, but warm you up.

Orecchiette con Rafano
(Orecchiette with Horseradish)

Paola (Sabatiello) Ignico, Bella, Potenza

Orecchiette is homemade pasta typical to Southern Italy. Its name is derived from its resemblance to a small ear (ear = orecchio and small = etto). Pasta dough (pages 306-7) is rolled out into long ¾-inch rolls, and cut into 1-inch lengths. Press down on the piece with your index finger and roll it towards you, making it curl. Then, turn it over and press your thumb down, pushing out the sides to make the indent bulge.

(Yield: 4 servings)

1 pound orecchiette	freshly ground pepper
salt	horseradish (peeled)
4 cups meatless tomato sauce (see page 308)	Romano or Parmigiano cheese

1. Bring pot of salted water to boil, add Orecchiette and cook until al dente.

2. Drain and return to pot, adding half of tomato sauce. Mix well.

3. Divide equally into 4 pasta plates, season with pepper, top with remaining sauce, grate fresh horseradish and freshly grated cheese.

In regards to your liking of horseradish, the more you grate the more you cry.

Peperoni Ripieni con Vino Cotto
(Stuffed Peppers in Cooked Wine)

Maria (Gruosso) Mecca, Ruoti, Potenza

As a teenager, my mother (Caterina) used to make this recipe. In those days vegetables were preserved in clay pots with a mixture of water, vinegar and salt. When the wine season came around they took freshly squeezed juice, usually red, and boiled it until it reduced to a quarter of the original amount to make "vino cotto."

(Yield: 4 servings)

4 preserved whole peppers
4 cups red wine (reduced to 1½ cups)
½ cup sugar
¼ cup extra-virgin olive oil

1 onion (diced)
½ cup golden raisins
3 cups coarse breadcrumbs

1. Cook wine and sugar in saucepan over medium heat until reduced to ¼ of original amount. Set aside (vino cotto).

2. Warm half the oil in skillet over medium heat and sauté onions until translucent. Add raisins and reserved vino cotto, stirring well. Cook for 3 minutes.

3. Add breadcrumbs to skillet, stirring until everything is mixed but still moist. Remove from heat, allow to cool to room temperature and reserve.

4. With sharp knife, remove stem from tops of peppers and clean out seeds and membranes. Try keeping stem hole as small as possible.

5. Fill each pepper with cooled mixture, pressing lightly as you fill cavity.

6. In the same skillet, warm remaining oil over medium heat and cook stuffed peppers, turning often on all sides, (approx. 15 minutes in total).

Serve with crusty Italian bread.

If preserved whole peppers are not available, fresh bell peppers can be substituted. Varying the colour adds a nice presentation.

Patate Arrosto con Peperoni Secchi
(Roasted Potatoes and Dried Peppers)

Maria (Ignico) Gugliotta, Bella, Potenza

Living on a small farm, a garden was absolutely necessary. I remember this recipe of my mother's because of the peppers. I was 8 years old and my mother sent me out to pick some peppers, stressing not to pick the hot ones, but the sweet ones. I knew what the peppers looked like, but the difference between hot and sweet? So I picked a pepper and took a bite. I ran back with a fire in my mouth, crying, and begging for sugar and water to put out the fire. After that, mother decided to pick them herself. —Tony

(Yield: 4 servings)

5 potatoes (peeled and cut into even wedges)

1 teaspoon salt

1 teaspoon freshly ground pepper

1 teaspoon paprika

4 tablespoons extra-virgin olive oil

1 teaspoon chili flakes (optional)

3 dried large sheppard peppers (broken up)

1. In large bowl add potato wedges, salt, pepper, paprika, 3 tablespoons of olive oil, chili flakes and toss until potatoes are fully coated with seasoning.

2. Grease 9x13 oven dish and add potatoes and bowl drippings. Roast on lowest rack of an oven preheated to 375°F for 20 minutes.

3. Lower oven temperature to 350°F, add broken pieces of dried peppers, give everything a good stir and continue roasting for another 20 minutes.

4. Potatoes are ready when crispy and can be pierced easily with a fork.

Remove, sprinkle with salt and serve immediately.

If dried sheppard peppers are not available, use fresh ones, cleaned and cut into ½-inch strips.

CALABRIA

CAPITAL
Catanzaro

RED WINE
Ciró

WHITE WINE
Greco di Bianco

Valle D'Aosta

Piemonte

Lombardia

Trentino-Alto Adige

Veneto

Friuli-Venezia Giulia

Liguria

Emilia-Romagna

Toscana

Marche

Umbria

Lazio

Abruzzo

Molise

Campania

Puglia

Basilicata

Calabria

Sardegna

Sicilia

Ligurian Sea

Adriatic Sea

Tyrrhenian Sea

Mediterranean Sea

Ionian Sea

Rigatoni alla Silana
(Rigatoni Silana Style)

Rita (Lia) Di Salvo, Sersale, Cosenza

(Yield: 4 servings)

1 pound rigatoni pasta
SAUCE:
4 tablespoons extra-virgin olive oil
17 ounces San Marzano or Roma tomatoes (diced)
½ cup onion (diced)
2 garlic cloves (minced)
1 tablespoon each finely
chopped parsley and basil
¼ pound capicollo (diced)
¼ pound Italian sausage
(casing removed and diced)

2 ounces pancetta (diced)
½ cup dried porcini mushrooms or 3 cups fresh
(chopped)
1 hot chili pepper (finely diced))

salt and freshly ground pepper
water as required
5 tablespoons grated Pecorino cheese
½ cup Mozzarella or Caciocavallo cheese (diced)

1. Warm oil in large skillet over medium heat. Add ingredients for sauce. Once boiling, season with salt and pepper; reduce heat to simmer and continue cooking for approx. 2 hours. Add water if the sauce looks dry.

2. In last 10 minutes, add pasta to large pot of salted boiling water and cook until al dente. Drain (reserve some of cooking water) and add pasta to skillet with sauce. Mix well. Add some reserved liquid if sauce is too thick.

3. Remove skillet from heat, add Pecorino and Mozzarella cheeses, and re-mix.

Serve topped with more Pecorino cheese.

Salsicce e Rapini
(Sausage and Rapini)

Teresa (Covelli) Pugliese, Aprigliano, Cosenza

Prior to the 1950s, meat was very expensive throughout Italy, and not everyone could afford it. Most families would raise their own pigs and use every part of it in some way or another. With other leftovers came the sausage and we, along with other families, would make our own for this dish. —Stella (Pugliese) Occhinero

(Yield: 4 servings)

4 Italian sausage links 5 to 7 inches (your favourite)

5 tablespoons extra-virgin olive oil

2 garlic cloves (chopped roughly)

1 head rapini (cleaned and drained)

1½ cups of water

salt and freshly ground pepper

1. Warm oil in medium skillet over medium heat and cook garlic until fragrant (30 seconds).

2. Add rapini and ½ cup of water with pinch of salt and cook until wilted.

3. Lower heat and simmer for 10 to 15 minutes.

4. Remove rapini from skillet and set aside.

5. Increase heat to medium, add sausage links and remaining water. Cook, turning sausage a few times.

6. When water has completely evaporated, cut links to 2- to 3-inches and return to skillet. Cook for another 5 minutes.

7. Return rapini to skillet and cook for another 3 minutes. Season to taste.

Serve warm on a plate together. Also excellent on a fresh Italian bun.

Zucchini o Fiori Fritti
(Fried Zucchini Rounds or Flowers)

Giovanna (Rocca) Acquafredda, Lamenzia Terme, Catanzaro

(Yield: 4 servings)

12 zucchini flowers or
2 medium zucchini* cut
into ¼-inch (or thicker) discs
1 cup flour
½ cup grated Parmesan cheese

3 eggs
½ cup white wine (or water)
extra-virgin olive oil
salt and freshly ground pepper

1. In bowl mix flour, cheese, eggs and wine until smooth, like pancake batter.

2. Warm oil in large skillet over medium-high heat.

3. Gently coat zucchini slices with batter and fry until golden. Flip over and fry other side.

4. Remove and place on paper towel to absorb excess oil.

5. Set onto serving plate; season with salt and pepper immediately and sprinkle with Parmesan cheese.

Serve warm.

*We used zucchini rounds for this recipe since a similar zucchini flower recipe can be found on page 145. Flowers are only available seasonally, but zucchini is available year round.

Minestra di Funghi
(Mushroom Soup)

Francesca (Gentile) Lia, Sersale, Catanzaro

This is a recipe that was taught and handed down to me by my mother. —Rita

(Yield: 4 servings)

3 tablespoons extra-virgin olive oil
1 onion (finely sliced)
6½ cups Porcini mushrooms (sliced)
2 cups peeled tomatoes (14 ounce can)
1 green sweet pepper (diced)

4 cups chicken broth (warmed)
1/8 teaspoon freshly ground pepper
salt
½ day-old Calabrese loaf (cut into large cubes)

1. Warm oil in saucepan over medium heat and cook onions until translucent.
2. Add mushrooms and cook for another 5 minutes. Add tomatoes and peppers; continue cooking until boiling. Add broth and freshly ground pepper and reduce heat to simmer (add more broth if you like).
3. Cook for another 10 minutes and re-season.
4. Arrange 4 bowls filled with cubed bread and ladle soup into each so bread is covered.

Serve hot.

Polpette di Ricotta
(Ricotta Balls)

Ersilia Dalia (Perrone) Gri, Motta Santa Lucia, Catanzaro

Here is one of those recipes that have been handed down through the generations. Paolo Dattilo received this from his mother (above) and she originally received it from her mother, Angela Perrone.

(Yield: 24 golf-size balls)

2½ pounds Ricotta
4 large eggs
2 cups breadcrumbs
1 tablespoon freshly ground black pepper

2 cups fresh parsley (finely chopped)
3 cups salami (diced)
1 cup grated Parmesan cheese
8 cups chicken broth or more (warm)

1. In large bowl add Ricotta, eggs, breadcrumbs, pepper, parsley, salami, cheese and combine thoroughly.

2. Layer cookie sheet with wax paper.

3. Using ice-cream scoop, measure portions of mixture. Roll into golf ball-sized rounds. Place balls on cookie sheet.

4. Meanwhile, warm chicken broth in large saucepan over medium heat.

5. Once broth has come to boil, drop in one layer of Ricotta balls.

6. When balls rise to surface they are cooked. Removed and set aside.

Serve warm with soup, by themselves, or at room temperature as a snack.

Zuppa di Patate con le Bietole
(Potato Soup with Swiss Chard/Spinach)

Rita (Lia) Di Salvo, Sersale, Catanzaro

This is one of those true peasant soups made with anything available at the time, usually from personal gardens.

(Yield: 4 servings)

2 tablespoons extra-virgin olive oil
2 medium onions (diced)
1 pound potatoes (diced)
8 cups of water

salt and freshly ground pepper
1 pound Swiss chard or spinach
(chopped roughly)
Pecorino or Grana Padano (optional)

1. Warm oil in medium saucepan over medium heat.

2. Add onions and cook until translucent. Add diced potatoes and cook for approx. 5 minutes.

3. Add water, salt and pepper (to taste). Allow to boil, then reduce to simmer.

4. Cook until potatoes are tender. Add chard/spinach and cook for another 5 to 6 minutes.

5. Re-season to taste.

Serve hot in individual bowls, sprinkled with Pecorino or Grana Padano cheese.

To add a little more flavour, you could substitute chicken broth in place of the water.

Bistecca alla Pizzaiola
(Steak in Tomato Sauce)

Mary (Piccolo) Radwick, Windsor, Ontario

This is the basic recipe for the very popular *Italian Bistecca alla Pizzaiola*. You can enrich it with ingredients such as chopped parsley (added a minute before serving), or a thin slice of Mozzarella cheese as a topping (added in the final stages of cooking). Some other recipes call for onions with tomatoes, among other things. For me, the basic recipe is enough and also very good!

(Yield: 4 to 6 servings)

4-6 beef steaks ($^3/_8$-inch thick,
your choice of cut)
4 tablespoons extra-virgin olive oil
salt and freshly ground pepper
2 garlic cloves (minced)

1 teaspoon dried oregano
5 ripe tomatoes (diced)
1½ tablespoons tomato paste
½ teaspoon hot red chili flakes

1. Warm 3 tablespoons oil in large skillet over medium heat.
2. Add steaks and brown each side. Add salt, pepper, garlic and sprinkle 1 teaspoon of oregano over steaks.
3. Once other side has browned, turn again and cook for another 3 minutes.
4. Remove steaks and cover with foil to keep warm.
5. In same skillet add remaining oil, tomatoes, tomato paste, oregano, salt, pepper and chilies. Adjust heat to high, scraping all brown bits and pieces left by meat. Cook 10 minutes until all tomatoes are completely incorporated.
6. Return steaks to skillet, making sure to cover with sauce. Put lid on skillet and cook for another 3 minutes.

Serve immediately.

Zuppa di Lenticchie con Salsiccia
(Lentil Soup with Sausage)

Francesca (Gentile) Lia, Sersale, Catanzaro

This is a recipe that was taught and handed down to me by my mother. —Rita

(Yield: 4 servings)

3½ tablespoons extra-virgin olive oil
8 Italian sausages (cut 1½ inches long)
3 cups lentils
2 garlic cloves (minced)

2 celery stalks (diced)
1 small carrot (diced)
2 bay leaves
20 cups water (warmed)
salt and freshly ground pepper

1. Warm ½ tablespoon of oil in skillet over medium heat and cook sausage pieces for 8 minutes. After sausages have rendered their fat, remove from skillet and set aside.

2. Warm remaining oil in large saucepan over medium heat. Add lentils, garlic, celery, carrots and bay leaves. Stir well and cook for approx. 3 minutes.

3. Add water and season with salt and pepper. Once boiling, reduce heat to simmer and cook for another 20 minutes.

Serve hot with toasted Calabrese bread.

Spaghetti con Fettine di Vitello
(Veal Fettine with Spaghetti)

Pina (Ventura) Olivito, San Giovanni in Fiore, Cosenza

(Yield: 4 servings)

1 pound spaghetti
2 tablespoons extra-virgin olive oil
½ cup white wine
1 pound veal fettine
(cut thin and sliced in ½-inch strips)
4 tomatoes (peeled and mashed)

1 small onion (sliced thin)
1 garlic clove (minced)
¼ cup fresh basil (finely chopped)
¼ cup fresh parsley (finely chopped)
salt and freshly ground pepper
grated Parmesan cheese

1. In large pot of salted boiling water, cook pasta until al dente.

2. While pasta is cooking, warm oil in large skillet over high heat, add wine, and fast fry veal strips (2 minutes per side). Remove and set aside.

3. Using same skillet, reduce heat to medium and add tomatoes, onions, garlic, basil and parsley. Season with salt and pepper and cook for approx. 5 minutes.

4. Return veal strips back to skillet and cook for another 2 minutes.

5. Drain pasta and add to skillet mixing thoroughly. Cook for 1 minute.

6. Remove skillet from heat, add good handful of cheese and re-mix.

Serve immediately. Top with more cheese.

Insalata di Patate alla Paesana
(Cold Potato Salad)

Franca (Rocca) Martinello, Lamezia Terme, Catanzaro

(Yield: 4 servings)

10 medium potatoes (cleaned and scrubbed)

½ cup sun-dried tomatoes

½ cup mixed olives pitted (green, black, etc)

1 red onion (thinly sliced)

1 cup cherry tomatoes (cut in half)

3 tablespoons extra-virgin olive oil

3 teaspoons white vinegar

salt and freshly ground pepper

1. In large pot of salted boiling water, add potatoes (skin on).

2. When potatoes are fork-tender, drain and run under cold water.

3. Cube potatoes into bite-size pieces and place in large bowl.

4. Add sun-dried tomatoes, olives, onions, cherry tomatoes and oil. Toss gently.

5. Add vinegar 1 teaspoon at a time (to taste). Season with salt and pepper.

Serve at room temperature.

Zuppa di Ceci
(Chickpea Soup)

Concetta (Lia) Rizzo, Sersale, Cosenza

(Yield: 4 servings)

SAUCE:
3 tablespoons extra-virgin olive oil
1 small onion (diced)
1 celery stalk (diced)
1 garlic clove (minced)
1 teaspoon rosemary leaves

5 fresh tomatoes or 1 15-ounce can (diced)
2 cups fresh chickpeas* or 1 19-ounce can (drained)
4 cups chicken broth

~

½ pound tagliolini egg noodles
chili flakes (optional)

1. Warm oil in large saucepan over medium heat. Add onion, celery, garlic and rosemary. Cook until onions are translucent.

2. Add tomatoes and continue cooking until tomatoes are cooked (approx. 8 minutes).

3. Add chickpeas and broth. Cook for another 3 minutes.

4. While preparing sauce, bring large pot of salted water to boil and cook egg noodles.

5. When noodles are al dente, drain and add to sauce, mixing well.

Serve hot, adding chili flakes if desired.

*If you are using fresh chickpeas, soak in water day before and then boil until tender.

Pittelli
(Fried Potato Fritters)

Ersilia Dalia (Perrone) Gri, Motta Santa Lucia, Catanzaro

(Yield: 20 pittelli)

3 pounds potatoes (peeled, boiled and mashed)

¾ cup grated Parmigiano-Reggiano cheese

3 teaspoons salt

½ cup fresh parsley (finely chopped)

¼ teaspoon black pepper

3 large eggs

¾ cup flour

canola oil

1. In large bowl combine cooled mashed potatoes, salt, pepper, flour, cheese, parsley and eggs.
2. Warm a saucepan with 1½ inches oil over medium heat.
3. Using large spoon scoop out a portion of mixture and with help of second spoon gently place in oil.
4. Fry pittelli until golden. Using spider remove and place on paper towels.

Season with salt while still hot and serve as warm appetizer with a dipping sauce of your choosing.

Polpette Calabrese con Sugo di Pomodoro

(Calabrese Meatballs in Tomato Sauce)

Maria (Pantuso) Martino, Pietrafitta, Cosenza

(Yield: 12+ golf-sized balls)

2½ cups cubed Calabrese bread
1 cup milk (or water)
2 pounds lean ground pork
½ cup breadcrumbs
3 eggs
½ cup grated Parmesan cheese

¼ cup finely chopped Italian parsley
1 teaspoon salt
1½ teaspoons freshly ground pepper
4 tablespoons vegetable oil
12 cups homemade tomato sauce (see page 308)

1. In small bowl, soak cubed bread in milk for approx. 10 minutes, then squeeze out liquid and add bread to larger bowl.

2. Combine with ground pork and breadcrumbs. Then combine with eggs, cheese, parsley, salt and pepper. Mix thoroughly.

3. Layer cookie sheet with wax paper. Set aside.

4. Portion mixture with ice-cream scoop, roll into golf-ball-sized rounds, and place on sheet.

5. Warm half the oil in skillet over medium heat. Fill with 1 layer meatballs.

6. Fry until golden brown. Remove and place on paper-lined dish. Fry remainder of meatballs with remaining oil.

7. Warm large saucepan of homemade tomato sauce over medium heat and place meatballs in sauce, covering balls completely.

8. Once boiling, reduce heat, and simmer partially covered for approx. 1 hour.

Serve with your favourite pasta, alone, or on a meatball sub!

Fagiolini al Pomodoro
(Long Flat Beans in Tomato Sauce)

Pina (Ventura) Olivito, San Giovanni in Fiore, Cosenza

(Yield: 4 servings)

3 tablespoons extra-virgin olive oil

1 pound flat green beans (trimmed)

2 large tomatoes (peeled and diced)

½ onion (diced)

1 garlic clove (minced)

1 cup water (white wine)

salt and freshly ground pepper

¼ cup parsley (finely chopped)

7 basil leaves (finely chopped)

1. Warm oil in large skillet over medium heat.

2. Add beans, tomatoes, onions, garlic, water (wine), salt and pepper. Cook covered for approx. 20 minutes. If dry, add more water (wine).

3. Remove from heat. Add parsley and basil. Toss until mixed.

Re-season and serve hot as a side dish.

A sprinkle of chili flakes adds great flavour to this dish.

Pasta Frittata

Teresa (Bossio) Naccarato, Amantea, Cosenza

This was a favourite at the dinner table, prepared by my mother. It can be made using fresh pasta (which my mother normally did) or leftover pasta. Both are fantastic.

(Yield: 4 servings)

1 pound pasta (spaghettini, capellini or vermicelli)
1 dried Italian sausage (4- to 5-inch links)
4 eggs

¼ pound Ricotta cheese
3 tablespoons extra-virgin olive oil
salt
Parmigiano cheese

1. Bring large pot of salted water to boil, add pasta and cook until al dente.

2. While pasta is cooking, remove skin from sausage and cut into thin slices. Set aside.

3. In bowl, beat eggs until nice and fluffy and set aside.

4. When pasta has cooked, drain and allow to cool.

5. In large bowl combine pasta, sausage, eggs, and Ricotta. Stir thoroughly.

6. Warm oil in large non-stick skillet over medium heat. Add pasta mixture. Cook until bottom is lightly toasted. Flip and toast other side.

7. Place on serving plate, cut into pizza-like wedges, and sprinkle with freshly grated Parmigiano.

Serve immediately.

Long thin pasta is great for this dish, but you can use any pasta or a mixture of several kinds. Remember to save that leftover pasta.

Baccalà in Salsa Marinara
(Cod in Marinara Sauce)

Maria (Mazzotta) Naccarato, Amantea, Cosenza

(Yield: 6 servings)

2½ pounds dried cod
MARINARA SAUCE:
3 tablespoons extra-virgin olive oil
1 onion (diced)

1 celery stalk (diced)
28 ounces plum tomatoes (crushed)
1 teaspoon finely chopped oregano
4 basil leaves
salt and freshly ground pepper

1. Prepare dried baccalà as per page 306 and cut into thick pieces.

2. Warm oil in saucepan over medium heat. Add onions and celery. Cook until onions are translucent.

3. Add tomatoes, oregano and basil leaves plus salt and pepper to taste. Cook for 30 to 40 minutes, stirring often.

4. Cover bottom of deep oven dish with sauce.

5. Place cod evenly in dish and top with remaining sauce.

6. Bake in oven preheated to 400°F for approx. 30 minutes. If fish separates easily with fork it is ready.

Place fish on a serving platter topped with the sauce, garnish with fresh basil, and serve.

Melanzane Ripiene
(Baked Stuffed Eggplant)

Anna Marie (Amato) Mancina, San Giovanni in Fiore, Cosenza

(Yield: 8 servings)

8 small Italian eggplants
STUFFING:
¼ cup extra-virgin olive oil
1 pound ground pork
1 pound ground veal
2 garlic cloves (minced)
¼ cup finely chopped fresh parsley
4 cups tomato sauce

2 cups breadcrumbs
¼ cup grated Romano cheese
1 egg, lightly beaten
¼ cup shredded Mozzarella cheese
salt and freshly ground pepper
oregano (to taste)

Romano cheese

1. Cut eggplants in half lengthwise. Remove and reserve pulp, leaving shell ¼-inch thick. Avoid tearing sides or bottom.

2. In large pot of boiling water, cook eggplant pulp for 15 minutes. After 10 minutes add shells to pot, drain, chop pulp and set aside.

3. Warm oil in skillet over medium heat, add ground meats, and brown lightly. Add the eggplant pulp, garlic, parsley and cook for approx. 20 minutes. Add half of the tomato sauce and continue cooking for another 15 minutes, stirring often.

4. Remove from heat and cool to room temperature. Once cooled combine with breadcrumbs, Romano cheese, egg and Mozzarella. Add salt, pepper and oregano to taste.

5. Lightly salt eggplant shells and fill with stuffing.

6. Layer baking dish with tomato sauce and place stuffed eggplants alongside each other. Pour remaining sauce over eggplants. Sprinkle with Romano cheese.

7. Cover baking dish with foil and bake in oven preheated to 375°F for 45 minutes. Remove foil and bake uncovered for an additional 15 minutes.

Serve hot or at room temperature topped with shredded Mozzarella cheese.

SARDEGNA

RED WINE

Cannonau di Sardegna

WHITE WINE

Vermentino di Gallura or Vernaccia di Sardegna

Spaghetti con Carciofi e Bottarga
(Spaghetti with Artichokes and Bottarga)

Luigi Marras, Guspini, Oristano

Artichokes are a major product of Sardinia. They're grown in winter, and are widely used in recipes all over the island. This recipe comes from the south of Sardinia, where the other local product is Bottarga.

(Yield: 4 servings)

5 baby artichokes
2 tablespoons extra-virgin olive oil
1 garlic clove (sliced thin)
½ cup water

salt and freshly ground pepper
1 pound spaghetti
¼ cup chopped fresh parsley
Bottarga (for garnish)

1. Clean artichokes. Remove hard outer leaves and cut in half. Slice halves thinly (the heart will keep them from breaking apart).

2. Warm oil in large skillet over medium heat. Add garlic and artichokes and cook for 3 minutes. Add water, season with salt and pepper, and cook covered for approx. 15 minutes. Add extra water to keep moist.

3. While artichokes are cooking, bring large pot of salted water to boil, add spaghetti and cook until al dente.

4. Drain pasta and add to saucepan. Allow to simmer for 1 minute, mixing thoroughly. Remove from heat.

Garnish with parsley and grated Bottarga (if available). Serve immediately.

Zuppa Gallurese
(Gallurese Soup)

Lisa (Corda) Codina, Windsor, Ontario

I lived in Arzachena, Olbia-Tempio, for 4 years. I taught English and acquired a taste for the local cuisine. One of my favourites was this recipe, which locals prepared to use up stale bread. *Zuppa* in Italian refers to a broth in which you soak bread to thicken it. Zuppa Gallurese isn't actually a soup – more like a cross between lasagna and casserole.

(Yield: 8 servings)

6 cups beef or lamb broth
stale Italian bread (sliced 1-inch thick)
1 garlic clove (peeled)
½ pound shredded Pecorino Fresco
freshly ground pepper

½ pound grated aged Pecorino Stagionato
or Parmigiano cheese
½ pound shredded Fontina (or any soft cheese)
¼ cup Italian parsley (chopped fine)

1. Bring broth to boil, cover with lid, and set aside.

2. Toast bread under broiler, remove and rub with garlic clove for flavour.

3. In bowl combine parsley, shredded Pecorino Fresco and pepper to taste.

4. Layer bottom of 7x10 oven dish with bread. Sprinkle half of Pecorino Fresco mixture and aged cheeses. Repeat. Top with layer of bread.

5. Ladle hot broth into dish until bread is wet but not soaked (once baked there should be no broth running at bottom of dish). Sprinkle top with Fontina.

6. Bake in oven preheated to 375°F for approx. 15 minutes or until all cheese has melted and is golden in colour.

Serve immediately.

Zucchine Ripiene
(Stuffed Zucchini)

Giacomina (Corda) Marras, Arzachena, Olbia-Tempio

Summer in Italy brings an overabundance of vegetables. Just about everybody has a garden. This recipe is one way of disposing of the surplus and at the same time keeping calories and fat to a minimum.

(Yield: 4 servings)

STUFFING:
4 white zucchini (cut in half lengthwise)
3 slices day-old Italian bread (grated coarse)
1 cup grated Pecorino (or Parmigiano)
½ cup corn
3 sun-dried tomatoes (chopped)
¼ cup parsley (finely chopped)
2 garlic cloves (minced)
1 onion (diced)
3 eggs (beaten)
salt and freshly ground pepper

2 tablespoons extra-virgin olive oil

1. Scoop out zucchini and reserve pulp.

2. In pot of salted boiling water, cook zucchini shells for 10 minutes.

3. In bowl combine pulp, bread, cheese, corn, sun-dried tomatoes, parsley, garlic and onion. Mix thoroughly.

4. Add eggs, mixing again. Season with salt and pepper. Set aside.

5. Remove zucchini shells with slotted spoon. Once cooled, dry thoroughly and fill with stuffing.

6. Place zucchini in oil-coated oven dish and sprinkle with cheese.

7. Bake in oven preheated to 375°F for approx. 20 minutes or until lightly golden in colour.

Serve warm.

Spaghetti di Mare al Zafferano
(Spaghetti Seafood with Saffron)

Teresa Manca, Palau, Olbia-Tempio

(Yield: 4 servings)

2 pounds clams (scrubbed and cleaned)

4 pounds mussels

1 pound spaghetti

2 tablespoons extra-virgin olive oil

2 garlic cloves (minced)

2 sun-dried tomatoes

¼ cup fresh parsley (chopped fine)

1 cup dry white wine

salt and freshly ground pepper

4 small saffron pouches

Pecorino cheese, grated

Bottarga, grated (optional)

1. Place clams and mussels in hot skillet; cook covered until they open (approx. 10 minutes). Discard any clams or mussels that have not opened.

2. Remove meat from shells (reserve a few in their shells) and set aside. Drain liquid through a fine sieve and reserve.

3. Bring large pot of salted water to boil. Add spaghetti and cook until al dente.

4. While pasta is cooking, warm oil in large skillet over medium heat and cook garlic until fragrant (30 seconds). Add reserved liquid, sun-dried tomatoes, parsley, clams, mussels, reserved shells, and wine. Cook until the alcohol has evaporated (approx. 3 minutes).

5. Season to taste. Add saffron and stir well.

6. When pasta is ready, drain and add to saucepan, mixing thoroughly.

Serve with a few of the reserved shells, freshly grated cheese and grated Bottarga (if available).

Zuppa di Pesce Senza Spine
(Boneless Fish Soup)

Giovanna (Lasia) Corda, Ozieri, Sassari

As a kid growing up in Sardinia we ate fish regularly and one recipe I liked was fish soup. Unfortunately one day I got a bone stuck in my throat and I refused to touch fish soup with a ten-foot pole. So my mother reinvented it, using only crustaceans and molluscs, telling me "Eat son, there are no bones in the soup." Hence the name. —Paul

(Yield: 4 servings)

¼ pound squid
¼ pound octopus
3 tablespoons extra-virgin olive oil
2 onions (sliced thin)
¼ pound lobster (meat)
¼ pound crab (meat)
3 anchovies

½ teaspoon chili flakes
2 tablespoons finely chopped fresh parsley
1 teaspoon finely chopped basil
salt and freshly ground pepper
10 cups tomato sauce
¼ pound cuttlefish
¼ pound shrimp

1. In pot of boiling water cook squid and octopus for approx. 15 minutes. Drain and chop into 1-inch pieces. Set aside.

2. Warm oil in large saucepan over medium heat; cook onions until caramelized (approx. 10 minutes). Add lobster, crab, anchovies, chili flakes, parsley and basil. Season with salt and pepper and cook for 5 minutes.

3. Add reserved octopus, squid and tomato sauce. Bring to simmer.

4. Add cuttlefish and shrimp. Stir and continue cooking covered for 10 to 15 minutes.

Serve while hot with crusty Italian bread.

Sardinian lobsters are smaller than the eastern Canadian type, have small claws and were left whole when cooked. Seafood proportions can vary to your taste.

Melanzane al Forno
(Oven-roasted Eggplant)

Rosa Lasia, Ozieri, Sassari

Rosa is my aunt on my mother's side and when visiting we were treated to the fruits of her garden. This recipe was one of my favourites. —Paul

(Yield: 4 servings)

4 eggplants
2 garlic cloves (minced)
¼ cup parsley (finely chopped)
8 basil leaves (finely chopped)

6 sun-dried tomatoes (finely diced)
extra-virgin olive oil
salt and freshly ground pepper

1. Cut eggplants in half lengthwise, sprinkle with salt and allow to stand in colander for 1 hour to purge bitterness.

2. In bowl combine garlic, parsley, basil and sun-dried tomatoes. Mix thoroughly.

3. Rinse eggplants and pat dry. Score eggplants in mesh pattern and rub mixture into scores.

4. Oil an oven dish and insert eggplants. Season with salt and pepper. Drizzle olive oil on top and bake in oven preheated to 350°F for approx. 35 minutes, or until tops are lightly browned.

Serve either right out of the oven or at room temperature.

Agnello al Forno
(Roasted Lamb)

Gavina (Corda) Marchesi, Alghero, Sassari

Gavina and her husband own a farm on the outskirts of town where they raise lambs for market. Juniper and laurel (bay) are plentiful there.

(Yield: 4 servings)

2 pounds lamb shoulder
(cleaned and cut into pieces)
MARINADE:
4 juniper leaves
4 bay leaves
1 bottle dry white wine

2 tablespoons extra-virgin olive oil
4 garlic cloves (minced)
4 big artichokes
salt and freshly ground pepper

1. In large bowl, mix lamb, juniper, bay leaves, and half the wine. Cover and marinate in refrigerator for 12 hours. Turn meat every few hours. Keep moist.

2. Remove, pat lamb dry, and discard marinade.

3. Warm oil in ovenproof Dutch oven over medium heat. Add garlic and cook until fragrant. Add lamb pieces and brown all sides.

4. Add cup of wine and continue cooking until alcohol has evaporated.

5. Place Dutch oven into an oven preheated to 325°F and roast for approx. 1 hour, uncovered, basting with juices and adding more wine if necessary to keep moist.

6. Meanwhile, prepare artichokes, removing tough outer leaves and trimming 1 inch from tops. Quarter. Add to lamb and continue roasting, covered, at 275°F for an additional 40 minutes. Baste often with juices.

7. Uncover and cook for another 10 minutes.

Serve hot by itself or with rice.

Panadas
(Sardinian Meat Pies)

Giovanna Palmas, Oschiri, Olbia-Tempio

Panada was one of my favourite meals back in Sardinia and I enjoy them every time I return. I still remember how my mother used to pack them for school lunches or for the "Merenda" (mid-afternoon snack). My favourite was the one stuffed with eels, which were plentiful in the area because of the lake.

(Yield: 12+ servings)

DOUGH:
2 pounds whole-wheat flour
(extra for kneading)
1 cup lard (plus extra)
1½ tablespoons salt
6 tablespoons lukewarm water (plus extra)

FILLING:
1 pound pork, lamb or freshwater eel
(small cubes)

1. Mix flour, lard, and salt in bowl for 2 minutes on low speed. Add water and continue mixing, adding extra water (1 tablespoon at a time if necessary), until dough comes together.

2. Remove from bowl and knead on lightly floured surface for a couple of minutes, then shape into ball. Cover with plastic wrap and allow to rest for 30 minutes.

3. Roll dough to thickness of no more than 1/16 inch. Cut out 6-inch rounds for pie base and 3-inch rounds for top. Re-wrap leftover dough and set aside.

4. Place strip of lard in centre of base.

5. Add meat cubes (or eel) over lard and then top with 3-inch round.

6. Lift the sides all around. Join to top and curl edges to seal top and bottom together. Pies are cooked in their own steam and must be sealed to preserve moisture of filling. Repeat with any leftover dough.

7. Place pies on cookie sheet and bake in oven preheated to 350°F for approx. 1½ hours or until golden.

For an interesting variation, combine ½ pound each of pork and lamb (or freshwater eel).

Anguilla al Pomodoro
(Freshwater Eel in Tomato Sauce)

Pasqua Barroccu, Tula, Sassari

(Yield: 4 servings)

2 pounds freshwater eel
(cleaned and skin removed)
flour for dredging
1 tablespoon crushed dry bay leaf
2 tablespoons extra-virgin olive oil

1 garlic clove (smashed)
2 tablespoons finely chopped parsley
1½ cups dry white wine
20 ounces crushed tomatoes
salt

1. Cut eel into bite-sized pieces and dry thoroughly. Dredge pieces in flour, sprinkle with crushed bay leaf and set aside.

2. Warm oil in skillet over medium heat, add garlic and parsley, and allow garlic to brown (approx. 3 minutes).

3. Remove garlic. Add eel and wine. Cook for approx. 5 minutes, turning pieces over. Remove eel and set aside. Keep warm.

4. Add tomatoes and bring to simmer. Season with salt and cook for 10 minutes.

5. Return eel to skillet and continue simmering, covered, for another 15 minutes.

Serve hot, topped with sauce, along with crusty Italian bread.

Because freshwater eel was not available, we used smoked eel and the results were excellent.

Sa Corda
(Skewered Innards)

Paul Corda, Tula, Sassari

In my youth back in Sardinia, at Christmas or Easter all the guys and girls would get together for an evening of feasting. We went to the nearest farm and ordered a lamb that the farmer would prepare and dress for us. Together, while the lamb roasted on a spit, we would make "Sa Corda" using the innards.

Ingredients from 1 lamb

innards (lungs, heart, liver, kidneys, pancreas, etc)
lining of abdomen
pancetta (very thinly sliced, if lining is not available)
intestines

10 garlic cloves (cut in half lengthwise)
extra-virgin olive oil
salt and freshly ground pepper
1 tablespoon rosemary (chopped fine)

1. Clean innards and lining thoroughly and set aside.

2. Clean intestines with salted water, then turn inside-out and wash again with salted water a few times.

3. Cut innards into 1½-inch cubes for skewering.

4. Skewer garlic and innards in alternation, ending with garlic. Repeat until all innards are used.

5. If available, wrap lining of abdomen around skewer (if not, use pancetta slices).

6. Wrap intestines tightly around skewer, criss-crossing one end to the other.

7. Drizzle some olive oil onto each skewer. Season with salt, pepper and rosemary. Grill over lowest heat until nice and crisp (approx. 20 minutes).

Serve with roasted lamb, Italian fennel, radishes (the long hot ones) and some artichokes.

SICILIA

CAPITAL
Palermo

RED WINE
Nero d'Avola

WHITE WINE
Insolia or Marsala

Pasta con le Sarde
(Pasta with Sardines)

Valeria Salerno, Siracusa

Last time I was back in Italy, visiting with my cousin in Pescia, we were treated to several wonderful dishes by his girlfriend Valeria Salerno. Valeria, who is from Siracusa, shared with us this traditional Sicilian dish with sardines. It is a simple dish, but is best made when sardines are fresh and in season. —Giuliano

(Yield: 4 servings)

1½ pounds bucatini pasta
1 cup fennel (chopped)
2 tablespoons extra-virgin olive oil
1 onion (diced)
½ pound fresh sardines (cleaned and deboned)

1 cup golden raisins
½ cup pine nuts
1 pinch of saffron
1 teaspoon salt
¼ cup of breadcrumbs

1. Bring large pot of salted water to boil and cook fennel for approx. 5 minutes. Remove fennel, set aside, and reserve water.

2. Warm oil in skillet over medium heat. Cook onions until golden. Add sardines, fennel, raisins, pine nuts, saffron and salt. Cook for approx. 10 minutes.

3. Re-boil fennel water and add pasta. When al dente, drain and return pasta to pot.

4. Add sardine mixture to pasta (with no heat), mixing thoroughly. Sprinkle in breadcrumbs and mix again.

5. In large oven casserole, bake pasta mixture in oven preheated to 350°F for approx. 5 minutes.

Serve immediately.

Risotto all' Arancia
(Risotto with Orange)

Anna (Palumbo) Duronio, Montallegro, Agrigento

This is a traditional Sicilian risotto that is perfect for vegetarians. The combination of orange zest and juice give it a nice citrus flavour that is not overpowering.

(Yield: 6 servings)

2 oranges (unblemished skins)
3 tablespoons extra-virgin olive oil
½ cup onions (minced)
2 tablespoons shallots (minced)
2 cups arborio rice

½ cup dry white wine
5½ cups chicken stock (heated)
2 tablespoons butter (cut into bits)
½ cup freshly grated Parmigiano-Reggiano
salt and freshly ground pepper

1. Using vegetable peeler remove rind from two oranges, being careful not to include pith (which is bitter). Cut rind crosswise into thin strips (½ cup). Juice oranges and reserve liquid (1 cup) along with rinds.

2. Warm oil in large skillet over medium heat. Add onions and shallots. Cook until golden.

3. Add rice and stir to coat with oil. Continue cooking until edges become translucent (1 to 3 minutes).

4. Add wine and orange rinds. Stir until wine is completely absorbed.

5. Add enough hot stock to moisten all rice plus ½ teaspoon salt, stirring constantly until all stock has been absorbed.

6. Continue to add stock in small batches, just enough to completely moisten rice again, and cook until each successive batch has been absorbed.

7. When all stock is absorbed, add orange juice. Stir constantly, adjusting heat level so rice is simmering gently, until creamy but al dente (30 minutes from time wine was added).

8. Remove from heat and stir in butter until completely melted. Add cheese and mix again.

9. Adjust seasoning with salt and pepper.

Serve immediately, in warm shallow bowls.

Crispeddi
(Anchovy Fritters)

Valeria Salerno, Siracusa

These little Sicilian snacks are eaten on market days or the saint's day of a town or village. They are perfect to share among friends and are great with drinks to start an evening. For the non-seafood lovers you can stuff them with Ricotta cheese and sun-dried tomatoes, rolling them into little balls so you can tell them apart.

(Yield: 12+)

DOUGH:
2½ cups flour
1 cup water
2 teaspoons dry yeast
3 teaspoons salt
3 tablespoons extra-virgin olive oil

FILLING:
anchovies (rinsed and filleted)
1 tablespoon oregano finely chopped
canola oil

1. Pile flour on work surface and form a well. In well, add water, yeast, salt and oil. Mix until dough starts to pull away from your hands.

2. Knead dough until smooth ball is formed (approx. 5 minutes).

3. Cover and place in draft-free spot, allowing 1 hour to rise.

4. Take piece of dough and flatten oblong. Fill centre with an anchovy and a pinch of oregano. Fold sides and ends. Pinch down to seal.

5. Set fritters on clean towel and cover, allowing ½ hour to rise.

6. Warm saucepan with 2 inches of canola oil over medium heat and fry a few crispeddi at a time.

7. When golden, remove with spider and set onto plate with paper towels. Sprinkle with a little salt while still hot.

Serve alone or with your favourite dip.

Melanzane Parmigiana alla Siciliana
(Sicilian Eggplant Parmesan)

Pietro Palermo, Gibellina, Trapani

Although there are many variations and ways to make eggplant Parmigiana, my husband prefers this traditional Sicilian method and recipe. —Kathy

(Yield: 6 to 8 servings)

3 large Sicilian eggplants
(washed, unpeeled)
MEAT SAUCE:
2 tablespoons butter
½ cup onion (diced)
2 garlic cloves (minced)
¼ teaspoon fennel seeds
¼ pound each ground beef, veal, pork
5 cups tomato sauce
14 ounces crushed tomatoes
¼ teaspoon freshly ground pepper
½ teaspoon chili flakes (crushed)

2 teaspoons dried oregano
1 teaspoon finely chopped basil
1½ teaspoons salt
1 tablespoon brown sugar

3 eggs slightly beaten
1 teaspoon water
¾ cup plain breadcrumbs
1½ cups Parmesan cheese
¼ cup extra-virgin olive oil
3 cups grated Mozzarella cheese

1. Prepare meat sauce by melting butter in large skillet over medium heat. Sauté onion, garlic and fennel seeds for approx. 3 minutes.

2. Add ground meat and cook for 5 to 8 minutes. Add remaining meat sauce ingredients. Simmer uncovered for 20 minutes, stirring occasionally.

3. Prepare two bowls, one with beaten eggs and water, and another with breadcrumbs and half a cup of Parmesan cheese. Set aside.

4. Slice eggplants crosswise (½-inch thick) and set aside.

5. Warm 1 tablespoon of oil in skillet over medium heat. Working in batches: dip eggplant slices into beaten egg mixture, dredge in breadcrumb mixture, and fry until golden on both sides. Place fried eggplants on plate with paper towels to remove excess oil. Continue frying eggplants, adding oil when necessary, until done.

6. In a pre-greased 9x13 baking dish, layer ½ of the eggplants.

7. Sprinkle Parmesan cheese, ladle ½ meat sauce and top with ½ Mozzarella cheese. Repeat with remaining eggplants, Parmesan cheese, and meat sauce. Bake uncovered in oven preheated to 350°F for 20 minutes.

8. Add remaining Mozzarella cheese on top and bake for another 20 minutes or until cheese is melted and slightly brown.

Pasta con Broccoli
(Penne with Broccoli)

Fina (Soresi) Frisella, Partinico, Palermo

(Yield: 4 servings)

1 broccoli head (cut in small pieces)
1 pound penne
2 tablespoons extra-virgin olive oil
1 onion (diced)

¼ cup pine nuts
½ cup golden raisins
14 ounces tomatoes (diced)
salt and freshly ground pepper

1. Bring large pot of salted water to boil and cook broccoli for approx. 3 minutes. Remove broccoli with slotted spoon and set aside, reserving water.

2. Add pasta to reserved water and cook until al dente.

3. While pasta is cooking, warm oil in large skillet over medium heat and cook onions, pine nuts, raisins and broccoli for approx. 5 minutes.

4. Add tomatoes to 1 cup of pasta water and cook for approx. 5 minutes or until pasta is al dente.

5. Drain cooked pasta and add to saucepan, cooking for another minute.

Season with salt and pepper and serve immediately.

Here is another truly hearty, flavourful vegetarian dish. Feel free to add your favourite green vegetables to this recipe.

Sarde a Beccafico
(Stuffed Fresh Sardines)

Joe Vesco, Alcamo, Trapani

This recipe has been in our family for generations. I do not know where my grandmother got it originally, but it has always been popular. The tails of fresh sardines roll up when they are cooked and resemble a bird called "Beccafico," which means "Fig-eater." It was considered a low-cost meal, because the sardines were not as expensive as other fish. Most of the ingredients were readily available in most homes, which made this recipe easy to prepare and cost-effective. It is now considered a delicacy and is served as an appetizer, but I still like it as a main meal after a dish of spaghetti.

(Yield: 4 servings)

2 pounds fresh sardines (heads removed)

FILLING:

1¼ cups breadcrumbs

½ cup grated Romano cheese

6 garlic cloves (minced)

2 teaspoons minced parsley

1 tomato (ripe and crushed)

2 tablespoons extra-virgin olive oil

1 egg (beaten)

1 teaspoon salt

½ teaspoon freshly ground pepper

1 cup flour

2 tablespoons extra-virgin olive oil

1. Debone sardines and butterfly. Rinse thoroughly under cold running water, pat dry and set aside.

2. In bowl, add all ingredients for filling and mix thoroughly.

3. Spoon mixture onto one side of opened sardine and fold shut. Repeat.

4. Dredge stuffed sardines on both sides in flour. Shake off excess and set aside.

5. Warm oil in skillet over medium heat and fry sardines, 5 minutes per side.

Serve immediately.

If fresh sardines are not available, a good substitute would be sole. Pine nuts and raisins may be added to the stuffing.

Arancine Siciliane
(Sicilian Rice Balls)

Angelina (Scalia) Milana, Montallegro, Agrigento

These were a favourite of my late husband Giovanni (Alcamo, Trapani). The only problem was trying to keep him away from them until they were all cooked.

(Yield: 20 to 30 tangerine-size balls)

2 cups long grain rice

1 pound each regular ground beef and pork (mixed together)

½ teaspoon oregano (dry)

1 tablespoon extra-virgin olive oil

½ cup onion (finely diced)

2 garlic cloves (minced)

5½ ounces tomato paste

1 pound peas
(fresh or frozen, not from a can)

1 cup each Romano and Parmesan cheese

4 cups breadcrumbs

¼ cup Parmesan cheese

salt and freshly ground pepper

5 cups canola oil

4 eggs (beaten)

1. Cook rice as per instructions on page 306 and set aside to cool.

2. Add oregano to combined ground meats, and remix, allowing a half hour to rest.

3. Warm oil in large skillet over medium heat and cook onions with garlic for approx. 3 minutes. Add seasoned ground meat and cook for another 7 minutes; add tomato paste and cook for 15 minutes more, until meat is done. Remove from pan and set aside to cool.

4. To saucepan of boiling water, add peas and cook for approx. 5 minutes. Drain and set aside to cool.

5. When all is at room temperature, add peas to meat, mix well and set aside.

6. Add 1 cup mixed cheese to rice. Mix well and set aside.

7. Form rice mixture into golf-ball sized balls. Create opening in centre with your finger and fill with meat. Close tightly and place on cookie sheet.

8. In shallow bowl combine breadcrumbs, Parmesan, salt and pepper to taste.

9. Warm canola oil in saucepan over medium heat.

10. Working with one ball at a time, coat with beaten egg and roll in breadcrumb mixture.

11. Carefully add to heated oil and deep fry until golden. Remove with spider and allow to drain on paper towels. Continue until complete.

Serve warm or at room temperature.

These can be eaten alone or covered with your favourite tomato sauce.

Couscous con Pesce
(Couscous with Fish)

Dina (Milana) Aiuto, San Vito Lo Capo, Trapani

Couscous is a Middle-Eastern food that was introduced to the Province of Trapani in the maritime area of San Vito Lo Capo following World War Two. Since fish was in abundance the local people introduced fish to the dish instead of chicken or pork (as was customary in Turkey during that time). Each year, San Vito Lo Capo hosts a Couscous Festival in mid-September.

(Yield: 4 servings)

1 cup couscous	water
4 fish fillets (5 ounces each)	6 parsley leaves
1 garlic head (peeled)	6 basil leaves
15 almonds	4 bay leaves
extra-virgin olive oil	shaving of cinnamon stick
1 onion (diced)	salt and freshly ground pepper
1 tablespoon tomato paste	flour

1. To food processor, add garlic, almonds and pinch of salt. Process for approx. 30 seconds. Add 1 tablespoon oil and process again for 30 seconds. Set aside.

2. Warm 2 tablespoons oil in saucepan over medium heat. Add onions, and cook until lightly golden.

3. Add tomato paste and 5 cups water (enough to eventually cover fish). Stir well.

4. Add parsley, basil, bay leaves and cinnamon shavings. Season with salt and pepper and ¾ garlic/almond mixture. Stir and bring to simmer.

5. Dredge fish fillets, shake off excess and set aside.

6. Warm 2 tablespoons of oil in skillet over medium-high heat and fry fish for approx. 1 minute per side (flouring/frying quickly helps keep fish together).

7. Add fillets and remaining garlic/almond mixture to saucepan when it begins to simmer.

8. Once fish is cooked (approx. 5 minutes) remove from saucepan and strain hot sauce into another dish. Add couscous, cover and allow to sit for approx. 10 minutes. Fluff couscous with fork.

Serve the couscous topped with a fish fillet.

Stufato di Agnello
(Lamb Stew)

Giacoma (Russo) Ferraro, Montallegro, Agrigento

(Yield: 4 servings)

2 pounds stewing lamb (1½-inch cubes)
1 cup white wine
2 garlic cloves (minced)
1 tablespoon rosemary leaves

¼ cup extra-virgin olive oil
salt and freshly ground pepper
1 red chili pepper (chopped, optional)

1. In a fridge-to-oven baking dish, combine all ingredients and mix well.

2. Seal dish with plastic wrap or tight lid and put in fridge to marinate for at least 2 hours (overnight is better).

3. Preheat oven to 350°F and remove dish from fridge. Give it another mix and discard plastic. Cover with aluminum foil.

4. Place dish in oven on middle rack and roast for 1½ to 2 hours.

5. After 1 hour of cooking, you can add optional red chili pepper.

Serve hot.

This dish is a drier stew and if you prefer you can add either more wine or water during the roasting process to keep it moist.

Bucatini con Melanzane
(Bucatini Pasta with Eggplant)

Anna (Caro) Buttice, Montallegro, Agrigento

Sicilian eggplants are normally round with a wide base and have purple skins streaked with white. They are sometimes referred to as Zebra or Graffiti eggplants.

(Yield: 4 servings)

4 small Sicilian eggplants
(peeled and halved lengthwise)
½ cup of salt (plus 1 tablespoon)
5 tablespoons extra-virgin olive oil
5 garlic cloves (roughly chopped)
5 cups tomato sauce

1 cup water
1 teaspoon chili flakes
1 teaspoon freshly ground pepper
6 medium basil leaves
1 pound bucatini pasta
Pecorino Romano cheese

1. Salt eggplant halves and set in colander to purge bitterness (approx. 1 hour).

2. Warm 2 tablespoons oil in saucepan over medium-high heat. Add garlic and cook until fragrant. Add tomato sauce, water, chili flakes, and pepper. Once boiling, reduce heat to low and simmer, partially covered, for 2 hours. Stir often.

3. Warm remaining oil in large skillet over medium heat, cook eggplants cut-side-down for approx. 8 minutes, turn, and cook other side until lightly browned. Set aside.

4. When sauce is almost finished, bring large pot of salted water to boil and add pasta.

5. Add eggplants and basil leaves to sauce.

6. When pasta is al dente, drain and return to pot, adding a little sauce.

7. Divide pasta into 4 servings. Top with sauce and 2 eggplant halves.

Serve with freshly grated Pecorino Romano cheese.

Carciofi Ripieni con Carne
(Meat-stuffed Artichokes)

Domenica (Scalia) Piazza, Montallegro, Agrigento

When I was growing up, my mother would make stuffed artichokes in the normal fashion using breadcrumbs, but on special occasions she would sometimes stuff them with meat. —Gino

(Yield: 6 servings)

6 medium-to-large artichokes

1 lemon quartered and juiced

STUFFING:

4 eggs (more if needed)

½ cup milk

1 cup seasoned or unseasoned breadcrumbs

¼ cup fresh basil (minced) or 1/8 cup dry

¼ cup fresh parsley (minced) or 1/8 cup dry

4 cloves of garlic (minced), more if you like garlic

½ cup grated Pecorino or Romano cheese

1 tablespoon salt

1 tablespoon freshly ground pepper

1 pound ground beef

28 ounces tomato sauce

1 cup water

1. Rinse artichokes well and cut bottom to sit flat. Trim 1 inch from top.

2. Snip tips of each leaf and remove any that are discoloured.

3. Using small knife or baller, scoop out choke and discard.

4. Place artichokes in large bowl filled with water, lemon quarters and juice (to preserve colour).

5. In bowl combine eggs, milk, breadcrumbs, basil, parsley, garlic, cheese, salt and pepper.

6. Add seasoning to ground beef and incorporate thoroughly.

7. Remove artichokes and allow to drain upside down on towels for 5 minutes.

8. Stuff meat mixture into centre of each artichoke and between as many leaves as possible. Then cup the top of each artichoke with meat and pack tightly.

9. Place artichokes into 9x12 oven dish or large Dutch oven until snug.

10. Combine tomato sauce and water, stirring thoroughly, and pour over artichokes. Almost cover.

11. Bake in oven preheated to 375°F for 1 to 1½ hours.

Serve while warm as a first course or together with your favourite pasta.

Ground pork or lamb in any combination can be used to stuff the artichokes.

Cannoli Siciliani
(Sicilian Cannoli)

Anna Piazza, Montallegro, Agrigento

While studying Italian at the Scuola di Italiano per stranieri in Lecce, we took cooking classes at a restaurant called *Il ristoro dei Templari* with Gianni Dell'Anna, the chef and owner. I told him I was Sicilian and my mother use to make Sicilian cannolis but I never could make them quite like her. He told me that his mother was Sicilian and that he would show me how his mother made them. He didn't just show me: his cooking classes were always "hands on." I made them and then took them home to my husband to try out. He loved them and so did I. Below is that recipe. Thank you Gianni!

2¾ cups pastry flour (250 g)
2 teaspoon each, cacao powder, vanilla, powdered coffee, cinnamon (5 g)
2½ tablespoons powdered sugar (20 g)
3 tablespoons lard, melted (40 g)
½ cup Marsala wine, more if necessary for consistency (100 ml)
1 small egg
4 cups sunflower or vegetable oil (1 litre)
Note: You will need a set of canoli tube tools to make shells.

FILLING:
1 pound fresh ricotta (454 g)
pinch of salt
1 tablespoon vanilla (15 ml)
2 teaspoons cinnamon (5 g)
1¹/3 cups sugar (250 g)
1 or 2 tablespoons maraschino cherry liquor (15 or 30 ml)
1 cup grated dark chocolate (100 g)
½ cup finely chopped pistachio nuts (50 g)
icing sugar for dusting

To make the shells:

1. Mix flour, cacao powder, vanilla, powdered coffee, cinnamon and sugar in bowl. Add melted lard and re-mix. Slowly add Marsala wine until it comes together (like bread), adding more Marsala as necessary.
2. Knead dough like bread, into an even consistency (not too soft, but not hard either).
3. Roll out into log and cut into 2 pieces, forming each one into ball. Let sit covered in plastic wrap at room temperature for 1½ hrs.
4. On floured surface, roll into 1/8-inch thickness and cut into square pieces for either the mini size or large size cannoli tubes and thin out one more time.
5. Beat egg in small bowl and set aside.
6. Place cannoli tube in middle of one of the dough squares, fold piece loosely around cannoli tube and brush end with egg mixture to seal. Continue until all the rolls are ready.
7. Heat oil to 160°C or 340°F in deep pot. Add few cannoli rolls at a time and make sure they are immersed in oil until golden brown (not burned).
8. Remove with spider and place shells on paper towels, allowing them to cool completely.

If you do not use canoli shells immediately, keep in a vacuum sealed box until ready to use. They will keep for months. Never store in the fridge as they tend to get soft and lose their crispness.

To make the filling:

1. Drain ricotta in colander in fridge overnight.
2. Using electric mixer, whip drained ricotta, salt, vanilla, cinnamon, sugar and cherry liqueur until smooth and fluffy. Fold in the grated chocolate and return to fridge until ready to use.
3. Using a pastry bag with a ½-inch hole, fill each cannoli shell with filling, dipping each end into the pistachio nuts. Dust with icing sugar.

Serve immediately.

Baci
(Italian Chocolates)

Norma (Sovran) Favaro, Windsor, Ontario

My husband Attilio would always come home with Baci chocolates, which were a favourite in our family.

(Yield: 200 chocolates)

1 pound shelled hazelnuts (454 g)

1 cup icing sugar (130 g)

½ cup unsalted butter at room temperature (115 g)

12 ounce jar Nutella or any hazelnut spread (340 ml)

2 pounds chocolate molding wafers or coating chocolate finely chopped (1 kg)

1. Spread hazelnuts on large cookie sheet and roast in oven preheated to 350°F for approx. 5 minutes. Once cooled, place hazelnuts in paper bag and shake to remove outer skins.

2. Grind hazelnuts in 1-cup batches in food processor or hand grinder. Continue until 1 cup coarse mixture is produced. Reserve balance of whole nuts.

3. Combine ground hazelnuts, icing sugar, unsalted butter, and Nutella in a bowl. Mix until ingredients are well-blended and set aside.

4. Place chopped chocolate in top bowl of double boiler.

5. Fill double boiler bottom with 1 inch water and bring to simmer.

6. Fit top bowl on boiler. Turn off heat once chocolate has melted.

7. Fill bon-bon moulds approx. ⅓ with chocolate and paint sides of mould with chocolate using small brush.

8. Place mould in freezer for approx. 5 minutes or until hardened.

9. Once hardened, place whole hazelnut in bottom of mould. Fill with reserved ground hazelnut mixture.

10. Cover with more melted chocolate, making sure whole top is covered.

11. Return mould back to freezer until hardened, then remove and set aside until ready to serve.

Tiramisu Classico
(Classic Tiramisu)

Carlo Negri, Tres, Trento

Tiramisu is one of the most common desserts prepared in-house, for its greediness and ease of execution. It is a decadent and sometimes complex dessert, since, depending on the execution, it can be very good or indigestible!

Today there are many variations that are lighter, but this is the classic recipe, whose origin is claimed by different regions. There are many legends concerning its invention, but the official purpose of this cake was to celebrate the triumphal entry of Grand Duke Cosimo III de'Medici in Siena at the end of the 17th century. The local pastry makers decided to invent a cake that reflected the character of the Grand Duke in its ingredients; hence the strength of the coffee and the simplicity of the ingredients composing this great dessert.

The Grand Duke liked this "Zuppa del Duca," so much, he brought the recipe to Florence, where, for its aphrodisiac properties they named it "Tiramisu."

(Yield: 6 servings)

5 fresh eggs (yolks and egg whites separated)

¾ cup sugar (150 grams)

pinch salt

1 pound Mascarpone cheese (500 grams)

½ cup Amaretto di Saronno (100 ml)

½ cup espresso (100 ml)

24+ ladyfingers (250 g)

2½ cups shredded dark chocolate (250 grams)

cocoa powder

1. Using electric mixer, beat egg yolks with sugar until thick and fluffy. Set aside.
2. Beat egg whites with a pinch of salt till stiff peaks form. Set aside.
3. Beat Mascarpone cheese until smooth and gently fold into egg whites.
4. Fold this mixture into egg yolks, creating a thick *crema*.
5. Mix Amaretto and espresso together and set aside.
6. Using a classic dessert glass, add a layer of *crema*, then a layer of ladyfingers. Spoon in some Amaretto/Espresso and then a second-leveled layer of *crema*.
7. Cover with chocolate shreds and repeat layering.
8. Finish with *crema*, a dusting of cocoa powder, and shredded chocolate.
9. Refrigerate for 2 to 3 hours before serving.

To make the cake version, you can use a single rectangular glass dish, following the steps above, making sure that the first layer is of ladyfingers.

Antipasto Veneto

Maria Frighetto, Liedolo di San Zenone, Treviso

Signora Frighetto was one of those ladies that always loved explaining "how to do it" when asked. She was the first to show me how to make fresh pasta and a few other recipes. One of the most flavourful appetizer recipes that she shared with me was her famous Antipasto Veneto. Whenever I called it "Signora Frighetto's Antipasto," she would correct me and state it was "Antipasto *Veneto*." She was just like that. —Gino

(Yield: approx. 22 small jars)

PRODUCE – Try to buy the following ingredients fresh:

6 to 7 carrots (cut into ¼-inch serrated discs)
1½ pounds beans, (yellow and green cut to 1 inch)
4 cups celery (½-inch cubes)
4 cups cauliflower (small florets)
3 each yellow, red and green peppers (cut ¾ x 1½ inches)
2 cups small white pickling onions

SHELF PRODUCTS:

4 to 6 cups white vinegar (1 to 1½ litres)
10 cups vegetable oil (2 litres)
3 cups tomato ketchup (750 ml)
13 ounces tomato paste (369 ml)
2 anchovy fillet packages (50 g each) in extra-virgin olive oil
1 jar pepperoncini peppers – 375 ml
1 jar fresh style gherkins – 375 ml
1 can pitted spanish black olives – 330 ml
1 can sliced green pizza olives – 375 ml
3 cans medium ripe black olives – 350 ml
1 can stuffed olives farcies – 244 ml
2 cans cebollitas cocktail onions – 370 ml or 2 cups fresh
1 jar capers – 105 ml
8 cans mushroom pieces & stems – 284 ml
6 cans solid white tuna in water (drained and broken up) – 133g
3 cans solid tuna in olive oil (broken up, undrained)

BLANCHING POT:

In pot bring vinegar to simmer.

ANTIPASTO POT:

1. Warm large pot that will hold 40+ cups, over medium heat. Add 8 cups of vegetable oil.
2. Add ketchup, tomato paste and anchovy fillets. Cook for approx. 10 minutes.

3. In another pot, set vinegar to boil. Blanch each vegetable listed for 3 minutes, drain and add each to oil pot.
4. Add broken-up chunks of tuna.

   NOTE: Keep oil level even with vegetables!

5. Cook for approx. 1 hour (total).
6. Fill each jar to top. Attach lids and finger tighten.
7. Preheat oven to 375°F.
8. Fill an oven roasting pan with approx. 1 inch of boiling water and place jars in pan.
9. Cook for another 30 minutes after jars begin to boil inside.

   NOTE: Jars are very HOT!

10. Remove jars from the pan and let rest upside down until cool.
11. Once they cool enough to handle, re-tighten lids.
12. Store for 3 months and enjoy.

Basic Procedures

Baccalà (Dry salted codfish)

• Best if soaked in water or milk for two days, changing liquid every 12 hours. This process does not need to be refrigerated.

• When you pick out a piece of baccalà remember that the colour of the meat should be close to white and the skin light-coloured. If the meat tends towards yellow, do not buy it.

• If sold whole, try to buy a long, thick fish; if possible it should be a bit more than 1-inch thick in the middle.

• If not already packed and wrapped in plastic, and you're allowed to smell it, remember that its odour, even if a bit intense, must be of fish and nothing else. No chemical smells should be evident.

• Prior to soaking, cut your baccalà into large pieces, which helps speed up the re-hydration process.

Besciamella Sauce (see ingredients note below)

1. In small pot, melt butter over medium-low heat.
2. Add flour and stir until smooth. Increase to medium heat and cook for 1 to 2 minutes (roux).
3. Meanwhile, heat milk in separate pot over medium heat until it begins to boil. Reduce to simmer.
4. Add butter mixture (roux) a little at a time to simmering milk, whisking continuously until very smooth. Bring to boil.
5. Cook for 2 to 3 minutes, stirring constantly, and then remove from heat. Season with salt, white pepper and nutmeg, and set aside until ready to use.
*Note: For thick Besciamella, use 2 tablespoons butter, 2 tablespoons flour and 1 cup milk. For **very thick** Besciamella, use 3 tablespoons butter, 5 tablespoons flour and 1 cup milk.*

Bread (Yield: 2, 1- pound loaves)

2 pounds flour
3 tablespoons salt
1½ tablespoons yeast
2 tablespoons extra-virgin olive oil
2 cups water (plus extra)

1. Using electric mixer on low speed, mix ingredients in order as above one at a time until each is fully incorporated.

2. Remove and cover, allowing to rise at room temperature for approx. 1 hour.
3. Divide risen dough and form two balls. Cover again and allow to rise for approx. ½ hour.
4. After second rise, form dough into loaf shape and allow to rise again for another ½ hour.
5. Place on lightly floured cookie sheet. Make three slits approx. ¼-inch deep along top of dough.
6. Bake in oven preheated to 350°F for 30 to 45 minutes or until a golden colour.
7. Allow to rest for 30 minutes. Slice and serve with a sprinkle of your favourite extra-virgin olive oil.

Cooking Rice (Yield: 4 servings)

1. Boil 2 cups of salted water in a pot. Add 1 cup of rice, stir once, then lower to simmer.
2. Cook covered for approx. 30 minutes or until water has evaporated.
3. Remove from heat, let stand covered for approx. 5 minutes. Fluff with fork and serve or set aside to cool.

Couscous (Yield: 4 servings)

1. In pot, bring 1½ cups of salted water to boil.
2. Stir in 1 cup couscous.
3. Remove pan from heat; cover and let stand for 5 minutes.
4. Transfer to bowl, fluffing with fork; let cool for 10 minutes.

Pasta (with eggs) (Yield: 4 servings)

Fresh Pasta with eggs for 1 pound of pasta
4 cups flour
1 cup water (plus extra)
4 eggs

1. Mound flour on clean working surface and make small well in the centre.
2. Add eggs and half of the water and bring flour in from sides a little at a time, slowly incorporating together.
3. Continue adding water as needed until the dough becomes slightly elastic but not sticky.
4. Knead dough for 10 minutes until incorporated and smooth.
5. Form into nice ball, seal in plastic wrap and allow to sit in refrigerator for 3 hours.

6. After it has sat, flatten the dough into a ¾-inch disc on a lightly floured surface.
7. Flour both sides of dough disc. Using a rolling pin, start in the centre and roll out the dough away from you and then towards you to the thickness required for the pasta you are making.
8. Cut or form into your desired pasta. Place on a lightly floured cookie sheet and cover until ready to cook.

Pasta (without eggs) (Yield: 4 servings)

Fresh Pasta without eggs for 1 pound of pasta
4 cups flour
1 cup water (plus extra)

1. Mound flour on clean working surface and make small well in the centre.
2. Add half the water and bring the flour in from the sides a little at a time, slowly incorporating together.
3. Continue adding water as needed until the dough becomes slightly elastic but not sticky.
4. Knead dough for 10 minutes until incorporated and smooth.
5. Form into nice ball, seal in plastic wrap and allow to sit at room temperature for 3 hours.
6. After it has sat, flatten the dough into a ¾-inch disc on a lightly floured surface.
7. Flour both sides of dough disc. Using a rolling pin, start in the centre and roll out the dough away from you and then towards you to the thickness required for the pasta you are making.
8. Cut or form into your desired pasta. Place on a lightly floured cookie sheet and cover until ready to cook.

Pasta (cooking)

Cooking pasta is easy, but following certain steps will ensure excellent results. The standard phrase used in this book to define cooked pasta is "al dente." Al dente, in the end is a matter of personal taste, but in general, indicates that the pasta should be firm, with a tiny white core in the centre.

1. Fill a large pot, using as a minimum ratio 1 quart (1 litre) of water per ¼ pound serving of pasta (100 g), and bring to a rapid boil. A little more water is always better.
2. Adding salt makes many recipes taste better. Use 1 tablespoon per gallon (4 quarts or litres) of water.

When the water comes to a rolling boil, add 1 tablespoon of coarse salt (a little less if it's fine-grained). The quantity in the end will be a matter of personal taste.

3. When the water is at a rolling boil, add pasta and give a good stir to keep from sticking. Adding oil is really not required to stop the pasta from sticking together. Stirring and stirring will take care of this on its own (oil makes the pasta slippery, and prevents sauce from sticking).
4. When water returns to a boil after adding pasta, start your timer. Most pre-packaged pastas will cook between 8 to 12 minutes as suggested by the manufacturer. If the water begins to foam, adjust the level of the heat.
5. Really the only way to tell if the pasta is correctly cooked is to taste it. It should be "al dente" – firm yet tender, with a tiny core in the middle as mentioned earlier.
6. Drain pasta into colander and lift, shaking off excess water. Don't rinse if you're serving a hot dish.

Tips:
• Never mix pasta types in one pot. Many have different cooking times.
• Watch the cooking process carefully. Pasta can overcook very quickly.
• If pasta is to be used in a casserole, cook it for half the time suggested. The cooking process will complete in the oven or skillet.
• Fresh pasta, especially egg pasta (fettuccine, tagliatelle, lasagna) cooks quickly, 3 to 5 minutes.

Pesto (Yield: ½ cup)

Normally a mortar and pestle is used, though a food processor does the job quite well.

1 cup fresh basil leaves
1 tablespoon pine nuts
2 garlic cloves
½ cup grated Parmigiano-Reggiano
¼ cup extra-virgin olive oil
Salt and freshly ground pepper

1. In a food processor, add basil and pine nuts and pulse a few times. Add garlic and pulse a few more times.
2. While processor is running, slowly add extra-virgin olive oil in a steady stream. Stop every once in a

while to scrape down sides and pulse until you have a liquid paste.

3. Season with salt and pepper to your liking.

4. Quantities and ingredients can be added and adjusted to suit taste.

Pie Dough (Yield: 2, 9-inch pie shells)

> 1 teaspoon salt
> 2/3 cup ice water
> 3 cups plus 2 tablespoons all-purpose flour, plus extra
> 1 cup plus 5 tablespoons very cold unsalted butter, cut into 1-inch pieces

1. In small bowl, mix together salt and water. Keep very cold until ready to use.

2. Place flour and butter in bowl of food processor. Pulse briefly until mixture forms large crumbs.

3. Add salt water mixture and continue pulsing until dough has just formed but is not smooth.

4. On a lightly floured work surface, evenly divide dough and form each piece of dough into a disc approx. 1-inch thick.

5. Wrap each disc in plastic and chill at least 2 hours or overnight.

Polenta (Yield: 4 servings)

> *(ratio: 4 cups liquid to 1 cup cornmeal)*
> 1 cup cornmeal (suggest medium yellow cornmeal)
> 4 cups water
> 1 tablespoon salt
> 1 tablespoon butter

1. In large pot, bring salted water to boil. Slowly pour in cornmeal, whisk until smooth, and quickly put the lid on for 2 to 3 minutes.

2. Remove lid and stir polenta constantly with a wooden spoon, turning by cutting the middle and bringing bottom to top. Stir for approx. 30 minutes.

3. Add butter and stir until fully blended.

4. If adding cheese, remove from heat, add cheese and continue stirring until thoroughly mixed.

5. Polenta is done when it comes away from the sides. Turn polenta onto wooden board or platter. Serve as-is or pour into any size pan or cookie sheet lined with parchment paper. Place in refrigerator to cool completely.

6. Once set, turn polenta out onto cutting board and cut into squares, rounds, or triangles.

7. Here you can fry, bake or broil to your liking.

Tomato Sauce (Yield: 12 cups or 3 litres/quarts)

> ¼ cup extra-virgin olive oil
> 1 carrot (diced)
> 1 onion (diced)
> 1 celery stalk (diced)
> 4 garlic cloves (minced)
> 1 can/2.84 litres whole tomatoes
> ½ cup basil (chopped)
> chili flakes (to taste)
> salt and freshly ground pepper

1. Warm oil in pot over medium heat. Sauté carrots, onions, and celery until tender (approx. 10 minutes).

2. Add garlic, cooking for another 2 minutes. Add whole tomatoes and basil. Season with salt, pepper and chili flakes. Once boiling, reduce heat and simmer 1 hour, stirring occasionally.

3. If rustic sauce is preferred, mash the tomatoes while they are cooking.

4. For a smooth sauce, place the contents into a food processor or blender.

Meat Sauce (Yield: 12 servings)

> 2½ pounds ground beef
> 2½ pounds ground veal
> 2½ pounds ground pork
> 1 tablespoon ground rosemary
> 4 garlic cloves (minced)
> 1 tablespoon ground sage
> salt and freshly ground pepper
> 3 tablespoons extra-virgin olive oil
> 12 cups tomato sauce (see above)
> 1 cup (250 ml) tomato paste
> 4 cups chicken broth

1. Mix all ground meats, rosemary, garlic, sage, salt and pepper in a large bowl.

2. Warm oil in large skillet over medium heat. Add meat mixture and brown, stirring occasionally.

3. Drain excess liquid. In large saucepan add prepared tomato sauce, tomato paste, chicken broth, and browned meat, cooking for 1 to 2 hours, stirring occasionally. Season with salt and pepper as required.

Conversion Tables

OVEN TEMPERATURES

FAHRENHEIT	225°	250°	275°	300°	325°	350°	375°	400°	425°	450°
CELSIUS	110°	120°	140°	150°	160°	180°	190°	200°	220°	230°

Measurements given below have been rounded for convenience.

WEIGHTS

IMPERIAL	METRIC
½ oz	15 g
1 oz	30 g
2 oz	60 g
3 oz	90 g
4 oz (¼ lb)	125 g
5 oz (1/3 lb)	155 g
6 oz	185 g
7 oz	220 g
8 oz (½ lb)	250 g
10 oz	315 g
12 oz (¾ lb)	375 g
14 oz	440 g
1 lb (16 oz)	500 g
1½ lb	750 g
2 lb	1 kg
3 lb	1.5 kg

LIQUIDS

IMPERIAL	METRIC
¼ cup	60 ml
1/3 cup	80 ml
½ cup	125 ml
2/3 cup	160 ml
¾ cup	180 ml
1 cup	250 ml
1½ cups	375 ml
2 cups	500 ml
3 cups	750 ml
4 cups	1 litre

LENGTHS

IMPERIAL	METRIC
¼ in.	5 mm
½ in.	1 cm
1 in.	2.5 cm
2 in.	5 cm
3 in.	7 cm
4 in.	10 cm
6 in.	15 cm
7 in.	18 cm
8 in.	20 cm
9 in.	23 cm
10 in.	25 cm
11 in.	28 cm
12 in.	30 cm

SPOON MEASURES

IMPERIAL	METRIC
¼ tsp	1.25 ml
½ tsp	2.5 ml
1 tsp	5 ml
1 tbsp	15 ml
2 tbsp	30 ml

Glossary

Al dente: Literally, "to the tooth"; refers to pasta, rice, beans and vegetables that have been cooked until tender though still firm, not soft.

Blanch: To plunge into a boiling liquid and cook 10 to 20 percent. This can also be used to remove the outer covering or skins from nuts, fruits, and some vegetables.

Boil: The process of bringing water or liquid to a boiling point; its surface is normally very agitated and rolling.

Bottarga: A dried salted roe from tuna or grey mullet (sometimes called the poor man's caviar), which can be obtained at most specialty food stores.

Capicollo: A salami made from pork shoulder or neck, and dry-cured whole.

Carpione: A style of cooking that uses vinegar and wine; also a marinating process.

Chiffonade: Any leaf vegetables or herbs cut into fine shreds and bunched together.

Chop: To divide into fine or rough pieces with a knife or other sharp tool.

Cube: To make a cube-shaped cut ½ to 1 inch.

Dice: A cube-shaped cut but smaller approximately ¼ inch.

Dredge: Refers to coating an item of food with flour, breadcrumbs, cornmeal, ground nuts, ...etc prior to cooking it.

Eggplant: Always buy eggplants that are firm and feel heavy for their size. There are two standard ways that are used to remove bitterness from eggplants after they have been sliced. One is to sprinkle salt on both sides and set in a colander for approx. 20 minutes. The other involves setting the eggplants in a bowl of salted water and allowing them to sit for approx. 30 minutes. After both methods, rinse off eggplants and thoroughly pat dry before using.

Farro (Spelt): After Julius Caesar's invasion of Egypt in 47 B.C., farro (emmer or spelt) came to Italy, the only country today where it is cultivated on a large scale. This nutritious grain became a staple in Roman society, sustaining the Roman Legions and even pro-

viding the root of the Italian word for flour: *farina*. Delicious and high in protein, over time farro saw its place at the table usurped by higher-yield, easily-harvested wheat. In recent years, farro has enjoyed a resurgence in popularity among gourmets and the health-conscious, who sing the grain's praises for its high nutritional value and adore the hearty, flavourful taste of the "Pharaoh's wheat."

Flour: In Italy, flour is classified either as 1, 0, or 00, which refers to the fineness of the grind and the bran and germ content. *Doppio zero* (00) is the most highly refined and is talcum-powder soft. **Frittata:** The Italian version of an omelette. Using egg as a base, together with a precooked vegetables, pastas, and meats, almost anything can be incorporated into it. This is normally turned, flipped or oven-baked and then cut into wedges.

Julienne: The process of cutting vegetables, potatoes, or other items into thin strips, 1/8 x 2- 3 inches.

Mortadella: An Italian cured sausage made of ground pork studded with pork fat. It can be spiced with black pepper, myrtle berries or coriander. Most mortadella that comes from Italy is studded with the pistachios or pine nuts native to its city of origin (Bologna); however those with flavours other than ground pepper and myrtle are not the original Bologna recipe. The best way to enjoy Mortadella is sliced very thin.

Pesto: Originating in Genoa, Italy, pesto is a sauce traditionally made of crushed garlic, basil and pine nuts blended with extra-virgin olive oil. There are many variants, and experimenting with your favourite herbs and spices can make your pesto personal and more exciting.

Ossobuco: Italian for "bone with a hole," a reference to the marrow hole at the centre of cross-cut veal.

Parmesan: This is often thought of as an English version of the word Parmigiano-Reggiano, but if a cheese is labelled "Parmesan," it merely imitates the recipe for Parmigiano-Reggiano without following D.O.C. laws. Typically a cheese labelled "Parmesan" has not been made in Italy. Within Italy, cheeses that imitate Parmigiano-Reggiano are called Grana (which means "granular" and refers to the texture). An example is Grana Padano.

Parmigiano-Reggiano: A cheese that follows Italian D.O.C. laws, which protect the names and recipes of certain cheeses. A cheese cannot be called Parmigiano-Reggiano unless it is made using a specific recipe and production method (normally within the provinces of Parma, Reggio-Emilia, Modena, and specific regions in the provinces of Bologna and Mantua). The D.O.C laws are meant to preserve the integrity of traditional cheeses, therefore, any cheese made outside of these regions with a slightly different recipe or production method cannot be called Parmigiano-Reggiano.

Parsley: There are only two types of parsley: curly and flat-leaf. Curly parsley has a pleasant grassy flavour and decorative ruffled leaves that make it the perfect garnish. When a stronger flavour is desired, recipes usually call for flat-leaf or Italian parsley, which features broad, serrated leaves.

Passatelli: A pasta formed of breadcrumbs, eggs, grated cheese, and nutmeg, cooked in chicken broth.

Passatutto: A food mill which is used for mashing and sieving soft foods. A passatutto typically consists of three parts: a bowl, a bottom plate with holes like those in a colander, and a crank fitted with a bent metal blade which crushes the food (forcing it through the holes in the bottom plate as the crank is turned).

Prosciutto Cotto: A delicately flavoured dry-cured ham, originating in Italy, made from the meat of the hindquarters of the hog. It is boiled prior to use.

Reduce: Refers to the continued cooking of a liquid until it reaches a smaller volume through evaporation. When this occurs, the liquid has a greater concentration of flavour. Adding starch allows it to become thicker.

Sauté: A method of cooking food quickly that uses a small amount of fat or oil in a shallow pan over medium to high heat.

Sculpit: A herb harvested from April to October, bordering cultivated land or found in the woods and in mountain pastures. The sprigs are harvested before blooming and used in cooking, mainly for pasta, meat, vegetables and salads.

Simmer: Cooking in a submerged liquid just below a boil. A simmering liquid has bubbles floating slowly from the bottom.

Skillet and Saucepan: Recognizing the differences between a frying pan (skillet) and a sauté pan (saucepan) isn't so tough. Both have flat bottoms and long handles. A skillet, with its low, sloping sides, is for food that needs to be stirred, scrambled, or flipped over, and a small amount of butter or oil is often used. A saucepan is for cooking the same food in the same keep-it-moving manner, but often with more liquid. It therefore often has deeper, steeper sides.

Speck: A flavoured ham originally from Tyrol, a historical region that since 1918 partially lies in Italy. Like prosciutto and other hams, speck is made from the hind leg of the pig, but, unlike other prosciutti, speck is deboned before curing, usually through a combination of salt-curing and smoking.

Translucent: When cooking onions translucent, the onion should be sort of clear at the edges but still a bit whitish in the centre. The onion should be soft. This usually this takes between 5 to 8 minutes, depending on the quantity.

Trippa: Edible organ meats from the stomachs of various farm animals.

Acknowledgements

What started as a simple keepsake has been transformed into a beautiful regional book containing a fine assortment of recipes. Representing all of the regions of Italy, our members, families and friends have provided us with an everlasting time capsule of over two hundred recipes for your enjoyment.

So many volunteers were involved in the production of this cookbook that it is difficult to know where to start. Giuliano Lunardi, Chairman of our Arts and Culture/Events Committee, was first approached about the idea. His support was overwhelming, then and now. With his assistance, the cookbook was presented and approved by the Giovanni Caboto Club Executive, Council and its Members.

Collecting, editing and translating these recipes was not an easy task, but was nevertheless accomplished by our group of dedicated volunteers. There are too many to list here, so we have dedicated the following page to listing all of them.

Collecting over 200 recipes is one thing, but it was our intention from the beginning to make, plate and taste each one. This became possible when our General Manager Ron Moro and Executive Chef Steven Ward and his team of cooks volunteered their services. The kitchen staff were incredible, preparing each recipe as they continued day-to-day operations servicing our members and their clients.

As the saying goes, a picture is worth a thousand words. We were fortunate to have an incredible photographer, Mauro Cechi, who photographed each recipe. Looking at his photographs alone would make one hungry.

Last but not least, we want to thank our members, families and the friends of our club who opened up their hearts and homes by supplying these recipes for all to enjoy.

I challenge all of you to try and test all of the recipes in this book. Most of all, I hope you enjoy them with family and friends!

Thank you to everyone!

Gino Piazza – Editor/Chair
Mauro Chechi – Photographer

Editorial Board:	**Cover and Design:**	**Sponsorship:**	**Translation Board:**
Joe Vesco	Mauro Chechi	Mauro Chechi	Laura Chechi
Mauro Chechi	Gino Piazza	Ron Moro	Mauro Chechi
Paolo Savio	Paolo Savio	Gino Piazza	Paolo Corda
Carlo Negri	Remo Tortola		Gino Piazza
Antonietta Piazza	Steven Ward		Paolo Savio
Gino Piazza			Dennis Segatto

Regional Advisory Board:

		Dessert Preparation:
Silvano Bertini	Frank Marceloni	Cristina Guelfo
Mauro Chechi	Carlo Negri	Antonietta Piazza
Paolo Corda	Pietro Palermo	Mauro Chechi
Nicola Di Salvo	Gino Piazza	Gino Piazza
Alessio Grilli	Paolo Savio	
Cristina Guelfo	Matthew Sgrazzutti	
Tony Gugliotta	Alessandro Sorrentino	
Giuliano Lunardi	Remo Tortola	

Submissions Board:

John Benotto, Veneto	Emilio Eugeni, Marche	Ron Moro, Friuli-Venezia Giulia
Silvano Bertini, Toscana	Angelo Ferraro, Sicilia	John Naccarato, Calabria
Filomena Bonato, Abruzzo	Alessio Grilli, Puglia	Carlo Negri, Trentino
John Bonato, Veneto	Tony Gugliotta, Basilicata	Pietro Palermo, Sicilia
Mauro Chechi, Lazio	Cristina Guelfo, Piemonte	Anna Piazza, Sicilia
Paolo Corda, Sardegna	David Hughes, Wales	Gino Piazza, Sicilia
Anthony Cutrone, Abruzzo	Giuliano Lunardi, Toscana	Paolo Savio, Friuli
Paolo Dattilo, Calabria	Caterina Lunardi (Latonna), Molise	Alessandro Sorrentino, Campania
Domenic Di Padova, Abruzzo	Frank Marcelloni, Umbria	Remo Tortola, Molise
Nicola Di Salvo, Lombardia	Carlo Luigi Mazza, Liguria	

Index

About the Editor

Although I was born in Italy, 50 years went by before I made my first trip back to the land of my birth.

It all began on one of those evenings around a table with my friends Graziano, Oliver, Mario, and Gary, among others, enjoying a few glasses of wine and discussing various wine-food pairings we enjoy, when the idea of a gastronomic/wine vacation to Italy was proposed. I agreed to go immediately, not just for the food and wine, but because this presented an opportunity to return to Italy.

Italy was absolutely beautiful and the effect of my exposure to its vast culinary diversity cannot be explained in words. Since that first trip I have been fortunate to make several more return visits, and cannot get enough of Italy. Every town, big or small, always amazes me with the diversity of food and the local wines that always compliment it.

I became so fascinated by Italian food that, once I retired, I took over the family kitchen entirely. After more than 25 years doing the cooking, my wife didn't offer a single word of argument.

When I proposed the idea of a regional cookbook to the Giovanni Caboto Club, their support was overwhelming. I have been fortunate to work with a fantastic group that have supported and assisted with this project and have made a dream we had come true.

Many thanks to all who assisted with *Cooking with Giovanni Caboto*. A special thank you goes to our Board of Directors, to Giuliano Lunardi (Chair of the Arts/Culture), and to our General Manager Ron Moro for his guidance throughout this project. Heartfelt thanks are also due Chef Steven Ward for bringing to life all of these wonderful flavours of Italy.

It goes without saying, Mauro, that I owe a deep debt of gratitude to you as well, both for your beautiful photographs and the friendship that we have gained in this process. —Gino.

Giacinto (Gino) Piazza was born in Montallegro, Agrigento, Sicily, Italy. His father waited in Canada for Gino's arrival, and he emigrated there, along with his mother and two sisters, in 1954. He received his Bachelor of Arts from the University of Windsor in 1984. He retired from the Canadian Broadcasting Corporation in 2000. Gino is married to Antonietta (Toni) and has two daughters, Jennifer and Deanna. He has been a member of the Giovanni Caboto Club since 2008.

About the Photographer

Mauro was born in Roma, Italy, in 1967. Following in his father's footsteps, in 1987 Mauro started his first business as a professional photographer in one of the most populated areas of Rome. In 1991 Mauro opened his second photography studio in Ciampino (a town close to Rome) after successfully completing a Master's degree in Large Format Photography at the Sinar Studio in Schaffhausen (Switzerland). In 1995 Mauro opened his third photography studio. Although his main focus has always been wedding photography, Mauro also worked with "still life," fashion, and commercial advertisements for important corporations such as Johnson&Johnson, Q8 Petroleum Company, RCL Shopping Bags, Orlandi Bath Systems, Atelier Luzzi Spose and Palombini Caffé. He also had the pleasure of working in the Cinecitta Studios with Dante Ferretti, the production designer and set decorator for *Gangs of New York* (2002) and *Cold Mountain* (2003). Since 2008 Mauro has been the official photographer for the famous Italian Chef Alessandro Circiello. More than twenty freelance photographers and videographers have contributed to the success of Mauro's business, helping him become very popular in Rome and across Italy. Mauro has always been interested in experimenting with new technologies in the field, and his first digital photo book was printed in 1997.

Two years later, in 1999, Mauro married his lovely wife Cristina. When their two children decided to begin their post-secondary education in Windsor, Canada, Mauro and his wife decided to accompany them on their new and fascinating adventure. In 2010 Mauro became a member of the Giovanni Caboto Club, where he had the opportunity to meet incredible people whom he now calls his friends and who, to some extent, have become his second family.

The realization of the Giovanni Caboto Club's cookbook has been an incredible experience for many reasons. Watching this project change and develop has been incredibly rewarding. It has also, however, involved great efforts and coordination on our part. The kitchen's staff has proved to be extremely professional, and it is only through the synchronization of multiple efforts that this book has been able to reach its potential. This project is also very ambitious, and I would never have thought that it could be completed in such a brief period of time. The nature of this project has made it one of the more challenging experiences of my career. However, collecting the recipes, translating them and finally transforming them into delicious dishes (which we then had the great pleasure of tasting . . . yummy!) was also very fun. Having my name associated with this book is truly an honor. I would like to extend my gratitude and thanks to all of those involved, and to the Giovanni Caboto Club as a whole, for having made my transition to Canadian life more pleasant, and for helping me broaden my professional horizons. —Mauro.

Good things come from Sysco®

Sysco, and the many companies we represent, are pleased that so many of our products are used in many of the recipes in this cookbook. We feel privileged to have been asked to support such a worthwhile and unique project. Well done!